Microwave Magic
International Cuisine

Grolier Limited
TORONTO

Contributors to this series:

Recipes and Technical Assistance:
École de cuisine Bachand-Bissonnette
Cooking consultants:
Denis Bissonette
Michèle Émond
Dietician:
Christiane Barbeau
Photos:
Laramée Morel Communications
Audio-Visuelles
Design:
Claudette Taillefer
Assistants:
Julie Deslauriers
Philippe O'Connor
Joan Pothier
Accessories:
Andrée Cournoyer
Writing:
Communications La Griffe Inc.
Text Consultants:
Cap et bc inc.
Advisors:
Roger Aubin
Joseph R. De Varennes
Gaston Lavoie
Kenneth H. Pearson

Assembly:
Carole Garon
Vital Lapalme
Jean-Pierre Larose
Carl Simmons
Gus Soriano
Marc Vallières
Production Managers:
Gilles Chamberland
Ernest Homewood
Production Assistants:
Martine Gingras
Catherine Gordon
Kathy Kishimoto
Peter Thomlison
Art Director:
Bernard Lamy
Editors:
Laurielle Ilacqua
Susan Marshall
Margaret Oliver
Robin Rivers
Lois Rock
Jocelyn Smyth
Donna Thomson
Dolores Williams
Development:
Le Groupe Polygone Éditeurs Inc.

We wish to thank the following firms, PIER I IMPORTS and LE CACHE POT, for their contribution to the illustration of this set.

The series editors have taken every care to ensure that the information given is accurate. However, no cookbook can guarantee the user successful results. The editors cannot accept any responsibility for the results obtained by following the recipes and recommendations given.

Canadian Cataloguing in Publication Data

Main entry under title:

International cuisine

(Microwave magic ; 24)
Translation of: La cuisine internationale.
Includes index.
ISBN 0-7172-2445-7

1. Microwave cookery.   2. Cookery, International.
I. Series: Microwave magic (Toronto, Ont.) ; 24.

TX832.C8413 1988   641.5'882   C88-094223-1

Contents

Microwave Magic is a multi-volume set, with each volume devoted to a particular type of cooking. So, if you are looking for a chicken recipe, you simply go to one of the two volumes that deal with poultry. Each volume has its own index, and the final volume contains a general index to the complete set.

Microwave Magic puts over twelve hundred recipes at your fingertips. You will find it as useful as the microwave oven itself. Enjoy!

Note from the Editor

How to Use this Book

The books in this set have been designed to make your job as easy as possible. As a result, most of the recipes are set out in a standard way.

We suggest that you begin by consulting the information chart for the recipe you have chosen. You will find there all the information you need to decide if you are able to make it: preparation time, cost per serving, level of difficulty, number of calories per serving and other relevant details. Thus, if you have only 30 minutes in which to prepare the evening meal, you will quickly be able to tell which recipe is possible and suits your schedule.

The list of ingredients is always clearly separated from the main text. When space allows, the ingredients are shown together in a photograph so that you can make sure you have them all without rereading the list—

another way of saving your valuable time. In addition, for the more complex recipes we have supplied photographs of the key stages involved either in preparation or serving.

All the dishes in this book have been cooked in a 700 watt microwave oven. If your oven has a different wattage, consult the conversion chart that appears on the following page for cooking times in different types of oven. We would like to emphasize that the cooking times given in the book are a minimum. If a dish does not seem to be cooked enough, you may return it to the oven for a few more minutes. Also, the cooking time can vary according to your ingredients: their water and fat content, thickness, shape and even where they come from. We have therefore left a blank space on each recipe page in which you can note

the cooking time that suits you best. This will enable you to add a personal touch to the recipes that we suggest and to reproduce your best results every time.

Although we have put all the technical information together at the front of this book, we have inserted a number of boxed entries called **MICROTIPS** throughout to explain particular techniques. They are brief and simple, and will help you obtain successful results in your cooking.

With the very first recipe you try, you will discover just how simple microwave cooking can be and how often it depends on techniques you already use for cooking with a conventional oven. If cooking is a pleasure for you, as it is for us, it will be all the more so with a microwave oven. Now let's get on with the food.

The Editor

Key to the Symbols

For ease of reference, the following symbols have been used on the recipe information charts.

The pencil symbol ✏️🍎 is a reminder to write your cooking time in the space provided.

Level of Difficulty

🍴 Easy

🍴🍴 Moderate

🍴🍴🍴 Complex

Cost per Serving

$ Inexpensive

$ $ Moderate

$ $ $ Expensive

Power Levels

All the recipes in this book have been tested in a 700 watt oven. As there are many microwave ovens on the market with different power levels, and as the names of these levels vary from one manufacturer to another, we have decided to give power levels as a percentage. To adapt the power levels given here, consult the chart opposite and the instruction manual for your oven.

Generally speaking, if you have a 500 watt or 600 watt oven you should increase cooking times by about 30% over those given, depending on the actual length of time required. The shorter the original cooking time, the greater the percentage by which it must be lengthened. The 30% figure is only an average. Consult the chart for detailed information on this topic.

Power Levels

HIGH: 100% - 90%	Vegetables (except boiled potatoes and carrots) Soup Sauce Fruits Browning ground beef Browning dish Popcorn
MEDIUM HIGH: 80% - 70%	Rapid defrosting of precooked dishes Muffins Some cakes Hot dogs
MEDIUM: 60% - 50%	Cooking tender meat Cakes Fish Seafood Eggs Reheating Boiled potatoes and carrots
MEDIUM LOW: 40%	Cooking less tender meat Simmering Melting chocolate
DEFROST: 30% **LOW: 30% - 20%**	Defrosting Simmering Cooking less tender meat
WARM: 10%	Keeping food warm Allowing yeast dough to rise

Cooking Time Conversion Chart

700 watts	600 watts*
5 s	11 s
15 s	20 s
30 s	40 s
45 s	1 min
1 min	1 min 20 s
2 min	2 min 40 s
3 min	4 min
4 min	5 min 20 s
5 min	6 min 40 s
6 min	8 min
7 min	9 min 20 s
8 min	10 min 40 s
9 min	12 min
10 min	13 min 30 s
20 min	26 min 40 s
30 min	40 min
40 min	53 min 40 s
50 min	66 min 40 s
1 h	1 h 20 min

* There is very little difference in cooking times between 500 watt ovens and 600 watt ovens.

A Ticket for a Gastronomic Trip

You don't know what to do with that jar of sauerkraut your sister-in-law brought back from her trip to Eastern Europe . . . For quite a while now you have been curious about how to prepare the fennel and leeks which are becoming more and more common in the fruit and vegetable section of the grocery store . . . You would like to serve something a little more exotic for supper. If you have been experiencing such culinary concerns, you are ready to explore international cuisine.

For both geographic and historical reasons, every region of the world has developed its own culinary tradition. This tradition is determined by the climate, by different forms of agriculture and, naturally, by the various local products. A country's or people's cooking is also affected by economic and political changes. Other important factors in determining particular gastronomy include migratory patterns and the discovery of new cultures. Socioeconomic conditions, whether propitious or unfortunate (in case of wars, supply difficulties or famine), can also cause significant changes in diet.

Improved means of communication and the virtually limitless exchange of information, broadened commercial exchanges, increased tourism and our own society's unfolding to the rest of the world have transformed our everyday cuisine, giving it a more international flavor. Italian spaghetti and Chinese chop suey are no longer considered exotic, and even such dishes as osso bucco and couscous are found in our recipe files.

This opening up to the outside world is simply an expression of our urge to explore. We enjoy discovering Hunter's Stew from Poland (page 46), Zucchini Greek Style (page 34) or the spicy flavor of the chili peppers served with many South American dishes.

It is just as much fun to rediscover some well-known foods prepared in new ways, such as Lebanese Meat loaf with Pistachios (page 62) or Rabbit with Coconut (page 80), a Venezuelan recipe that certainly would not have appeared in our grandmother's cookbooks. Curry, cumin, coriander, turmeric, saffron—these are some of the exotic spices whose secrets were largely unknown just a short time ago, and which we now feel more comfortable using in our own recipe.

Culinary tourism is also inexpensive, so don't hesitate any longer; invite your friends to a theme supper. After all, the best way to really get to know a country and to get a little closer to its people is by sampling its cuisine.

France

Italy

Greece

Germany

Eastern Europe

England

Your Gastronomic Itinerary

Cooking is an art that does not respect political frontiers; it is really more regional than national. Rice, for example, is an ingredient that is not limited to just one country but is the basic food of almost every oriental cuisine. In the same way, tomatoes are essential to many Mediterranean dishes, not just to those of a single country. For this reason, we have grouped the recipes in this volume according to broad geographic divisions.

France, the home of gastronomy on a grand scale, has the honor of being first of the list. Next comes Italy, a country of pasta, figs and prosciutto. We then travel to Greece and take in its mastery of the abundance of the sun and the sea.

Heading north, we pass through Germany on our way to Eastern Europe. Then we take a quick trip to England and, since the English were great explorers, we shall follow their example and explore the Middle East and then the Far East to sample the flavors of Egypt, Lebanon, China, Korea, Japan and Indonesia.

One of our last stops is in the sun-filled Central and South Americas. Our round-the-world trip returns to our point of departure, North

Middle East

Far East

South America

Scandinavia

United States

Quebec

America, but not without stopping in at the Scandinavian table, filled with dishes more similar to our own than we might have thought.

International cuisine is certainly an adventure. Fortunately, most of the ingredients required in the preparation of these dishes are easy to find. But if you can't find a particular food, substitutions are almost always possible. Of course, any substitution will modify slightly the flavor or the texture of the dish, but the substitutes we suggest are easily integrated into the original recipe.

Inevitably, many of the recipes presented here are adaptations since the microwave oven is not one of the traditional cooking methods of Egypt or Mexico! But there is nothing to worry about; Japanese-style carrots and bean sprouts are just as delicious and crunchy when cooked in the microwave oven and the aroma of Pork and Potatoes with Fruit Sauce (page 78) is just as enticing prepared in the microwave as it is prepared in the open air, under the Peruvian sky.

Microwaves and Foods

Microwave cooking is easy to master when you carefully follow the instructions and keep a few general principles in mind. For example, it is important to remember that the water or fat content of a food is what determines its cooking time. A food with a high water content, such as a tomato, will cook much more quickly in the microwave oven than a squash or an apple.

The shape of a food and the way it is arranged in the oven will also affect the way it cooks. A large piece of meat, such as a roast, should be placed in the center of the oven to ensure that it cooks uniformly. Irregularly shaped foods should be placed so that their fleshiest parts are toward the outside of the cooking dish, where the microwaves are more intense. In fact, in the case of poultry, you should sometimes cover the less fleshy parts such as the wings and drumsticks with aluminum foil to delay premature cooking.

You should also take into account the size of the pieces of food being cooked. A vegetable cut into uneven sizes will not cook uniformly; the smaller pieces will overcook and will lose some of their flavor and nutritional value.

For a long time the appearance of meat cooked in the microwave was faded and unappetizing because it was impossible to sear foods with this method of cooking. The only way around this problem was to brush sauces, such as soy sauce or Worcestershire sauce, over the surface of the food to give it color. However, these ingredients are not always suited to the food being cooked, so many people were tempted to return to the traditional oven. But a solution has since been found. The problem of browning is now a thing of the past: browning dishes for the microwave oven have been developed. These dishes, coated with ferrite, are specially designed to absorb the energy from the microwaves and, becoming very hot, are capable of searing food.

The chart opposite gives guidelines as to the power levels and the cooking times required for different types and quantities of foods. Note that for even cooking it is important to allow the standing times indicated.

A Guide to Cooking Various Foods

Food	Quantity	Power Level	Cooking Time (min)	Standing Time (min)
Meat and Fish				
Beef, steaks	1 large	100%	6 to 8	None
Chicken, pieces	1 kg (2.2 lb)	70%	22	5
Chicken, whole	1 kg (2.2 lb)	70%	22	10
Fish, breaded	450 g (1 lb)	100%	6 to 9	5
Fish, fillets	450 g (1 lb)	100%	3-1/2 to 6	2
Fish, whole		70%	6 to 9 min/lb	2
Ham		50%	12 min/lb	10
Lamb, chops	4	70%	5 to 7	None
Pork sausages	25 g (8 oz)	100%	4 to 6	2
Scallops	450 g (1 lb)	70%	5 to 7	2
Shrimps, shelled	450 g (1 lb)	70%	4 to 6	2
Spaghetti sauce	540 mL (19 oz)	100%	12 to 15	None
Turkey, whole		70%	13 min/lb	20
Vegetables				
Asparagus, spears	450 g (1 lb)	100%	3 to 4-1/2	3
Beans, green	225 g (8 oz)	100%	7 to 9	2
Broccoli, spears	450 g (1 lb)	100%	6 to 8	2
Brussels sprouts	450 g (1 lb)	100%	5 to 6	3
Cabbage, wedges	225 g (8 oz)	100%	6 to 8	2
Carrots, sliced	225 g (8 oz)	100%	7 to 9	3
Peas, fresh	225 g (8 oz)	100%	5 to 7	3
Spinach, fresh	450 g (1 lb)	100%	3 to 4	2
Pasta and Rice				
Macaroni	225 g (8 oz)	100%	7 to 9	None
Noodles	225 g (8 oz)	100%	6 to 8	None
Rice, brown	250 mL (1 cup)	100% / 70%	30 to 35	None
Rice, instant	250 mL (1 cup)	100%	4	2
Rice, long grain	250 mL (1 cup)	100% / 70%	14 to 16	5
Spaghetti	225 g (8 oz)	100%	6 to 9	None

Ingredients To Discover

Fruits and Vegetables

International cuisine opens the door to the unsuspected wonders of nature. There are so many fruits of earthly paradise beyond the apple available now to tempt us. Pineapples, kiwis, mangoes, avocados, coconuts, figs, mandarins, nectarines, papaya, apricots, quince, dates and pomegranates are some of the better-known fruits that we eat regulaly. But the lichee (with its white, pulpy flesh), the delicately perfumed mangosteen, the persimmon (which resembles a tomato), the plantain (a type of firm fleshed banana), the guava (with its delicious nectar) and the kumquat (a sort of miniature orange) may also one day equal the better-known fruits in popularity.

This expansion continues in the vegetable garden; it is just as abundant and as varied. Starting with endives, artichokes, snow peas and kohlrabi and adding yams (tubers used in the preparation of stews and soups and to make sweet dishes), bamboo shoots, vine leaves, yucca (an edible root rich in starch), manioc (a white fleshed root that is the basis of tapioca) as well as the many different types of legumes—we are hardly limited in our choices.

Seasonings—A Special Touch

The spices and herbs used by the chefs of all these different countries play a tremendous role in transforming our culinary habits. Dare to go beyond the everyday black or white papper and you will find a thousand delicious new seasoning agents. You will learn how to make better use of paprika, a seasoning incredibly rich in Vitamin C that enhances the flavor and color of so many dishes. You will renew your acquaintance with ginger and cinnamon, spices which may sit forgotten in your kitchen cupboard (see our recipe for Lebanese Meat Loaf with Pistachios, page 62). A little more curiosity and you can sample meat in a sauce seasoned with mace and potatoes flavored with nutmeg.

International cuisine will also encourage you to explore the many spices from India—curry, cumin, cayenne, cardamom, cloves, turmeric and saffron.

Herbs, fresh or dried, add subtle flavors to foods. The best known is certainly parsley, an aromatic plant which has the added advantage of being decorative. Thyme, bay leaves and mint are also commonly used in kitchens in most parts of the world.

In Mediterranean countries, popular herbs include garlic, marjoram (from the oregano family), rosemary (just a few sprigs are enough to flavor a dish), savory (an aromatic particularly suited to vegetables), thyme (and its cousin wild thyme), basil (an essential ingredient of the famous pesto) and tarragon.

Other herbs used in different countries include coriander (the leaves of which resemble parsley and have a very characteristic scent), sage, anise, (a favorite of the bakers and pastry chefs of Europe), caraway, (very popular in the East), the fragil chervil and dill, often used in marinades.

There is no product of nature that civilizations have not explored and exploited. But don't worry, you don't need to throw yourself into the adventure of sampling grilled shark steaks to discover international cuisine. The key to discovering a foreign cuisine is not so much in the preparation of complicated dishes made from unusual ingredients but rather in the unexpected blending of known ingredients. Today, the fruit of our ancestors' insatiable curiosity is within our grasp; enjoy it!

Hard To Find?

If cooking is a science, it is certainly a very flexible one. In fact, you will find in preparing the recipes in this volume that substitutes can frequently be used for the required ingredients. And if you are unable to find the substitute, certain ingredients can simply be omitted. Obviously, each ingredient contributes to the overall character of the recipe and its omission will certainly modify, to some extent, the texture or flavor of the dish. It would be unthinkable, for example, to omit the soy sauce in an oriental recipe and it would be a shame to leave out the water chestnuts, which add a fresh, crisp texture to many recipes. On the other hand, a Peruvian pork dish can easily be made without the few grains of annatto that might be listed in the recipe ingredients.

Some food substitutions are more common than others. A Chinese recipe calling for a few leaves of Chinese cabbage *(bok-choi),* also frequently used in Japanese cooking, can just as easily be made with Chinese lettuce or even romaine lettuce. If the recipe calls for Chinese allspice, which you certainly won't find at your corner store, you can use your own dependable allspice and the substitution will be neither seen nor tasted.

Substitutions for seasonings are relatively easy to make since, over the centuries, international commerce has opened up a vast trade in all sorts of spices. As a result, many combinations of spices exist in different forms, even in far-off countries. You shouldn't be surprised that cayenne pepper, which comes from the city of Cayenne in French Guiana is widespread in South America and is used in much the same way as the small, crushed red chili peppers.

Vegetable substitutions are a little trickier. Fortunately, some very exotic vegetables, such as yucca and chayote can be replaced, respectively, by the Jerusalem artichoke and the zucchini. But most vegetables have such a characteristic flavor that their omission would threaten the success of the dish.

Many exotic dishes call for fresh seafood, sometimes rather difficult if not impossible to find close to home. Here again, substitutions can be made. Snow crab, a type of North American crab sold in tins in most supermarkets, can replace crab meat. Likewise, the ricotta cheese called for in Italian recipes can be replaced by cottage cheese. You will also find that these two substitutions are less expensive. Local products, in fact, are often more economical than the more exotic ones. However, you should take advantage of these savings with caution; any substitution will modify the taste of a dish and detract in part from its authenticity.

France: The Empire of Fine Food

For centuries, different national cuisines have drawn inspiration from the traditions and methods of those in other parts of the world. As a result of conquests, invasions, expeditions and cultural exchanges, every country in the world has refined its way of preparing food. But no country has been as well able to integrate contributions from the outside or to demonstrate as much imagination in the kitchen as has France, the uncontested queen of international gastronomy.

France's reputation as the land of gastronomy was not born yesterday. In fact, except for a few ancient Greek texts dedicated to the culinary arts (of which, unfortunately, no trace remains), the first cook books date from the fourteenth century and are French. Since then, France's authority in gastronomic matters has not been challenged. Chefs there are revered as demi-gods. The most celebrated of all is undoubtedly Auguste Escoffier, called the king of chefs and the chef of kings for having served many crowned heads. He is the author of many cook books and the creator of many recipes, which he liked to dedicate to the great names of his time and to personalities in the artistic world. The *Peach Melba,* a famous dessert, was named in honor of a well-known singer and is probably the best known of Escoffier's creations.

It would be impossible to try to paint a picture of French cuisine in just a few lines. Its recipes range from Ardenne game to Amiens duck pâté. Cold cuts from the Alsace or Franche-Comté have been exported for years. The technique of cooking with wine was developed in Burgundy and then expanded to many other regions. Dijon is celebrated for its mustard, Lorraine for its quiche and pastries and Languedoc for its cassoulet Toulouse. France also produces a large variety of cheeses from almost every region of the country as well as wines which are unique in the world. Corsica happily adapted many Italian dishes and the cooking of Alsace is the envy of the Germans, whose cuisine inspired this region of France. Provence is well known for its flavorful dishes—its pizzas, called *pissaladières,* its *ratatouille* and its *bouillabaisse.* Brittany is unequalled in its preparation of shellfish, which does not prevent it from producing a profusion of crêpes as well. The Ile de France, which includes the well-stocked Parisian area, has seen the creation of a variety of special dishes that have become world famous, thanks to the work of some of the great chefs of the area. Depending on the region, French cooking can be simple or as sophisticated as the cooking of Imperial China or modern-day Japan, but its taste is always well defined.

Desserts are important everywhere in the country and there is one for every taste, from the Tarte Tatin to Crêpes Suzette or profiteroles.

Taking a trip to the heart of French gastronomy means experiencing a long and delicious adventure, full of tastes and satisfactions.

Cassoulet (France)

Level of Difficulty	🍴🍴 🍴🍴
Preparation Time	1 h*
Cost per Serving	$ $
Number of Servings	20
Nutritional Value	450 calories 28.9 g protein 30.2 g lipids
Food Exchanges	4 oz meat 1/2 bread exchange 2 fat exchanges
Cooking Time	5 h 5 min
Standing Time	None
Power Level	100%, 50%
Write Your Cooking Time Here	

* Soak the beans, salt pork, pork rind and pig's trotter in water with the fennel for 12 hours before cooking.

Ingredients
450 g (1 lb) navy beans
pinch fennel powder
115 g (4 oz) salt pork, cubed
225 g (8 oz) pork rind, cut into strips
1 pig's trotter, boned
45 mL (3 tablespoons) butter
3 onions, finely sliced
1 carrot, sliced
3 garlic cloves, finely sliced
45 mL (3 tablespoons) flour
625 mL (2-1/2 cups) beef consommé
1 bouquet garni
3 tomatoes, peeled and chopped
pinch saffron
4 Toulouse sausages
1 roast pork, 1.3 kg (3 lb), boned and pierced with slices of garlic
1 chicken, 1.3 kg (3 lb), cut into quarters
125 mL (1/2 cup) hot water

Method
— Combine the fennel, salt pork, pork rind and pig's trotter in a large bowl; add the beans and enough water to cover the mixture. Let soak for 12 hours.
— Cook these ingredients at 100% for 40 minutes.
— Remove the salt pork, pork rind and pig's trotter; set aside.
— Add enough water to cover the beans if needed and continue cooking at 100% for 30 minutes.
— Stir and continue cooking at 50% for 1 hour, stirring twice during the cooking time.
— Drain the beans and set aside.
— Put the butter in a dish and add the onions, carrot, garlic and pieces of salt pork; cover and cook at 100% for 4 to 5 minutes, stirring once during the cooking time.
— Sprinkle with the flour and mix well.
— Add the consommé, stirring constantly.
— Cover and cook at 100%

for 10 minutes, stirring twice.
— Add the bouquet garni and the tomatoes; continue cooking, uncovered, at 100% for 30 minutes, stirring twice during the cooking time.
— Strain the mixture through a sieve and add the saffron; set this sauce aside.
— Pierce the sausages in several places with a fork and cook at 100% for 5 minutes.
— Pierce the sausages again, reserve the fat and cut them into thick slices; set

aside.
— Preheat a browning dish at 100% for 7 minutes, add the fat from the sausages and heat at 100% for 30 seconds.
— Sear the roast pork on all sides.
— Add the pig's trotter, the chicken and the hot water.
— Cover and cook at 50% for 1 hour.
— Cover and cook at 50% for 1 hour.
— Remove the meat, reserving the cooking liquid, and cut the pork roast into thick slices.
— Put half the beans in the

bottom of a casserole and cover with the roast pork, chicken, sausages, pork rind and pig's trotter.
— Place the remaining beans on top and add the cooking liquid from the roast pork and the prepared consommé-based sauce.
— Cover and cook at 100% for 5 minutes; reduce the power to 50% and continue to cook for 1 hour, giving the casserole a half-turn halfway through the cooking time.

Rabbit with White Wine (France)

Level of Difficulty	🍴🍴
Preparation Time	45 min*
Cost per Serving	$ $
Number of Servings	6
Nutritional Value	457 calories 27.6 g protein 17.4 g lipids
Food Exchanges	3 oz meat 4 fat exchanges
Cooking Time	58 min
Standing Time	5 min
Power Level	100%, 70%
Write Your Cooking Time Here	

* Marinate the rabbit for 12 hours before cooking.

Ingredients
1 rabbit, 1.3 kg (3 lb)
250 mL (1 cup) white wine
50 mL (1/4 cup) olive oil
30 mL (2 tablespoons) wine vinegar
1 onion, finely sliced
2 mL (1/2 teaspoon) thyme
1 bay leaf
15 mL (1 tablespoon) parsley, chopped
salt and pepper to taste
115 g (4 oz) lean salt pork
12 pearl onions
15 mL (1 tablespoon) butter
1 clove garlic, crushed
3 green onions, chopped
15 mL (1 tablespoon) flour
125 mL (1/2 cup) chicken bouillon

Method
— Cut the rabbit into serving pieces.
— In a bowl, combine half the white wine, the oil, wine vinegar, onion, thyme, bay leaf, parsley, pepper and salt; add the rabbit and marinate for 12 hours in the refrigerator.
— Stir the pieces of rabbit several times.
— Cut the salt pork into cubes and put them in a dish; cook at 100% for 2 to 3 minutes, stirring once during the cooking time; remove the pork and set aside. Reserve the fat.
— Preheat a browning dish at 100% for 7 minutes.
— In the meantime, remove the pieces of rabbit from the marinade and dry them carefully; set the marinade aside.
— Put the cooking fat from the salt pork into the heated browning dish, add a little more oil if needed and heat at 100% for 30 seconds.
— Sear the rabbit on all sides; put the pieces into a casserole and set aside.

— Heat the browning dish at 100% for 4 minutes and sear the pearl onions; remove and set aside.
— Add the butter and heat at 100% for 30 seconds; add the garlic and green onions and heat at 100% for 1 minute.
— Sprinkle with the flour and mix well; add the remaining wine and the chicken bouillon.
— Cook at 100% for 3 to 4 minutes, stirring every minute.

— Pour the mixture over the rabbit; add the marinade and pieces of salt pork.
— Cover and cook at 70% for 20 minutes.
— Stir the pieces of rabbit and add the pearl onions.
— Cover and continue cooking at 70% for 20 to 30 minutes or until the meat is tender.
— Let stand for 5 minutes.

This exotic dish will no doubt satisfy the most demanding palates. These are the ingredients you will need.

Trout with Almonds (France)

Level of Difficulty	🍴
Preparation Time	10 min
Cost per Serving	$ $
Number of Servings	4
Nutritional Value	550 calories 43 g protein 40.1 g lipids
Food Exchanges	6 oz meat 2-1/2 fat exchanges
Cooking Time	13 min
Standing Time	4 min
Power Level	100%, 70%
Write Your Cooking Time Here	

Ingredients
4 trout, 340 g (12 oz) each
pepper to taste
60 mL (4 tablespoons) butter
75 mL (1/3 cup) sliced almonds
15 mL (1 tablespoon) parsley, chopped

Method
— Carefully rinse the trout, dry them and pepper the cavities.
— Preheat a browning dish at 100% for 7 minutes; add half the butter and heat at 100% for 30 seconds.
— Sear the trout; cover and cook at 70% for 4 minutes.
— Move the trout from the center of the dish to the outside and turn them over.
— Cover and continue cooking at 70% for 4 to 6 minutes.
— Let stand for 4 minutes.
— Put the almonds in a measuring cup and add the remaining butter; cook at 100% for 2 to 3 minutes or until the almonds are golden, stirring twice during the cooking time.
— Put the trout on a serving platter and garnish with the almonds and parsley before serving.

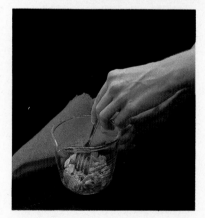

This simple but original recipe can be prepared in less than half an hour. First assemble these ingredients.

Move the trout from the center of the dish to the outside and turn them over after they have cooked for 4 minutes.

Stir the almonds twice during the cooking time to ensure even cooking.

Italy: Full-Bodied Delights

Just mention "Italian cooking" and it brings to mind the sumptuous banquets of ancient Rome, those feasts with innumerable courses and flowing wine. Some people will think of delicious pasta with thick sauces; others will recall the aroma of a pizza with a light crust, laden with slices of pepperoni and mushrooms. These gustatory and olfactory memories make us regret that we don't live in the center of the restaurant district of Naples.

However, Italian cuisine is not confined to pizza and pasta. First of all, the brief period of the Roman Empire, during which only the rich and powerful could indulge themselves day after day, was followed by several centuries of austerity. In fact only the Italian monks, isolated in their monasteries, could retain some vestige of the cooking of that time. The Muslim invasion in the ninth century gave Italian cuisine its second wind. With the arrival of these new conquerors, *gelati* and *cassata,* Neapolitan ice creams, appeared. During the Middle Ages, commercial travel brought a revolutionary new ingredient to the peninsula's tables: sugar. For a long time Venice served as the entry point for spices from the Orient and imported fruits and exotic vegetables.

It was also in the twelfth century that Chinese noodles first arrived in Venice. As we know, this food, brought back by Marco Polo, was to be very important to Italian cooking. Many other countries claim to have discovered pasta dough, but it was certainly the Italians who began to prepare pasta with its many sauces. And when Italians left their own country, they brought their pasta with them. Today it can be found all over the world. More than 325 different types of pasta are now made, from tagliatelle to tortellini, from ravioli to lasagna. Italians usually serve pasta at the beginning of the meal; the pasta is cooked *al dente,* meaning still slightly crunchy, but pasta can be prepared in many different ways.

Pizza is another dish the origin of which is probably not Italian, but Italians have adopted pizza as part of their diet and have taken it around the world with them. The popularity of this recipe, a thick dough-based crust garnished with tomato sauce and cheese, has spread from Naples to America.

Typical Italian cooking is also characterized by its clever use of vegetables, especially the tomato; this national vegetable (which in strict botanical terms, is really a fruit) is used throughout Italy. The southern sun matures the tomato until it is plump and juicy and it is used as the base for many sauces.

Meat is less widely used in Italian cooking but, where it is used, veal is king. Veal is prepared in many different ways: piccata with lemon, osso bucco, or escallops of veal with Marsala wine. Italians also enjoy a variety of cold cuts. An antipasto combining finely sliced Parma ham, melon, salami, mortadella and bresaola, a dried beef, is often served as an appetizer or as a light meal.

The Italian peninsula stretches into the Mediterranean, an inexhaustible source of seafood; prawns, tuna, swordfish and sardines regularly fill the fisherman's net.

Served with a bottle of Chianti or Valpolicella at room temperature, your Italian meal will surely be *delizioso!*

Osso Bucco (Italy)

Level of Difficulty	🍴
Preparation Time	20 min
Cost per Serving	$
Number of Servings	4
Nutritional Value	418 calories 27.2 g protein 4.6 mg iron
Food Exchanges	3 oz meat 2 vegetable exchanges 1/2 bread exchange 2-1/2 fat exchanges
Cooking Time	1 h
Standing Time	5 min
Power Level	70%
Write Your Cooking Time Here	

Ingredients
8 veal shanks
50 mL (1/4 cup) flour, toasted
50 mL (1/4 cup) oil
1 onion, finely chopped
125 mL (1/2 cup) celery, finely chopped
45 mL (3 tablespoons) parsley, chopped
1 carrot, grated
2 cloves garlic, crushed
1 540 (19 oz) can tomatoes, drained and chopped
125 mL (1/2 cup) dry white wine
250 mL (1 cup) chicken bouillon
5 mL (1 teaspoon) oregano
salt and pepper to taste

Method
— Dredge the veal shanks in the toasted flour.
— Preheat a browning dish at 100% for 7 minutes; add the oil and heat at 100% for 30 seconds.
— Sear the veal shanks.
— Add all the other ingredients and season.
— Cover and cook at 70% for 50 to 60 minutes, moving the shanks from the center of the dish to the outside halfway through the cooking time.
— Let stand for 5 minutes and serve.

Lovers of Italian food will enjoy this fine dish; these are the ingredients you will need to prepare it.

Flour the veal shanks and then sear them in a browning dish containing heated oil.

Add all the other ingredients and cook.

Move the shanks from the center of the dish to the outside halfway through the cooking time to ensure uniform cooking.

27

Prawn Risotto (Italy)

Level of Difficulty	🍴
Preparation Time	20 min
Cost per Serving	$ $ $
Number of Servings	4
Nutritional Value	524 calories 25 g protein 26.7 g lipids
Food Exchanges	3 oz meat 2 bread exchanges 3 fat exchanges
Cooking Time	52 min
Standing Time	5 min
Power Level	100%, 70%
Write Your Cooking Time Here	

Ingredients
450 g (1 lb) prawns
1 bay leaf, crumbled
2 cloves garlic, crushed
1 L (4 cups) hot water
75 mL (1/3 cup) softened butter
45 mL (3 tablespoons) olive oil
1 onion, chopped
500 mL (2 cups) long grain rice
50 mL (1/4 cup) white wine
salt and pepper to taste

Method
— Put the prawns, bay leaf, garlic and hot water into a casserole; cover and cook at 100% for 9 to 11 minutes.
— Remove the prawns, shell them and set aside.
— Put the shells into the cooking liquid and cook at 100% for 10 minutes. Remove the shells and set the liquid aside.
— Put the butter and oil into a dish; heat at 100% for 1 minute.
— Add the onion and the rice; cook at 100% for 4 to 5 minutes, stirring halfway through the cooking time.
— Stirring constantly, blend in the prepared prawn bouillon and the white wine.
— Cover and cook at 100% for 8 minutes and stir.
— Reduce the power to 70% and continue cooking for 15 to 17 minutes.
— Slice the prawns, add the rice and season to taste. Cover and let stand for 5 minutes.

These are the ingredients you will need to prepare this recipe, which will surely win you many compliments.

In a casserole, combine the prawns, bay leaf, garlic and hot water; cover and cook at 100% for 9 to 11 minutes.

Stir the mixture of butter, oil, onion and rice once during the cooking time.

Tagliatelle with Tomato Sauce (Italy)

Level of Difficulty	🍴
Preparation Time	20 min
Cost per Serving	**$**
Number of Servings	8
Nutritional Value	285 calories 11.4 g protein 34.9 g carbohydrate
Food Exchanges	1 oz meat 2 bread exchanges 1/2 vegetable exchange 1 fat exchange
Cooking Time	27 min
Standing Time	None
Power Level	100%, 70%
Write Your Cooking Time Here	

Ingredients
225 g (8 oz) egg tagliatelle (or fettuccine)
225 g (8 oz) spinach tagliatelle (or fettuccine)
1.5 L (6 cups) boiling water
5 mL (1 teaspoon) salt
5 mL (1 teaspoon) oil
115 g (4 oz) Parmesan cheese, grated

Sauce:
450 g (1 lb) Italian tomatoes
45 mL (3 tablespoons) oil
2 cloves garlic, crushed
5 mL (1 teaspoon) basil
pepper to taste

Method
— To make the sauce, peel, seed and coarsely chop the tomatoes.
— Put the oil and garlic in a dish and cook at 100% for 1 minute.
— Add the tomatoes, basil and pepper.
— Cook at 100% for 5 minutes.
— Stir and reduce the power to 70%; continue to cook for 10 minutes, stirring and breaking up the tomatoes with a fork twice during the cooking.
— Cover the sauce and set aside.
— Put the pasta into the boiling water with the oil and salt; cook at 100% for 7 to 9 minutes; stirring twice during the cooking time.
— Drain the pasta, arrange on a serving platter and add the sauce.
— Reheat at 100% for 1 to 2 minutes.
— Garnish with Parmesan before serving.

Pasta lovers will enjoy this easy-to-make dish. First assemble the ingredients shown.

Use a potato masher or a fork to break up the tomatoes twice during the cooking time.

Stir the pasta twice during cooking to prevent sticking.

Greece: Cooking Under the Mediterranean Sun

The Greek civilization is one of the oldest in the world. Greece is the cradle of Western civilization and the influence of its artists, writers and philosophers have determined our present civilization. However, typical Greek cooking has only recently become popular, and we are still familiar with only a few dishes, such as vegetable dishes, lamb kebabs and some desserts.

However, Greeks have brought a great deal to the world of cooking. For example, it was the Greeks who first developed the principles on which the science of dietetics is based. They were also the first to present awards for recipes to their chefs.

Greek cooking is characterized by the use of healthful foods, prepared as simply as possible in order to retain all their flavor and nutritional value. The people of this country, where the sun and the sea are omnipresent, are particularly fond of fish and vegetables.

Since the sheep population is significant, butcher meat is mainly mutton and dairy products are derived mainly from goats and sheep.

Greek cuisine makes substantial use of herbs and aromatic vegetables. Almost all recipes use saffron, fennel, oregano, cumin, coriander, anise, mint, garlic or onion.

Fish and meat dishes are usually prepared with olive oil, which Greece produces abundantly, and lemon juice—two ingredients that, along with the aromatic herbs, are found in almost every dish.

Greek cooking is distinguished also by its original method of preparing vegetables. This Mediterranean country grows eggplant, indispensable for its well-known moussaka, as well as zucchini, cucumbers, tomatoes and many other vegetables that are served stuffed, au gratin, puréed or marinated in olive oil and lemon juice. Vegetables

marinated in this way and served cold are typical of Greece and are now known all over the world.

Dairy products are equally abundant. Goat and sheep milks are used to make yoghurt and a variety of cheeses, of which the best known are feta and the very salty kephalotyri.

Alternately conquered and conqueror, Greece has been subjected to many foreign influences, acquiring a taste for very strong Turkish coffee and for rich, sweet oriental pastries.

As well, the large number of vineyards are the source of an important grape harvest and a successful wine industry. Aromatic herbs are also used in the preparation of liqueurs, such as anise, which gives us the celebrated ouzo.

The rustic style of Greek cuisine, full of Mediterranean sun and freshness of flavor, will undoubtedly please lovers of simple food.

Zucchini Greek Style

Level of Difficulty	🍴
Preparation Time	20 min*
Cost per Serving	$ $
Number of Servings	8
Nutritional Value	160 calories 1.1 g protein 0.6 mg iron
Food Exchanges	2 vegetable exchanges 2-1/2 fat exchanges
Cooking Time	21 min
Standing Time	None
Power Level	100%
Write Your Cooking Time Here	

* Once the zucchini is cooked, it should be left to marinate for 2 hours in the refrigerator before serving.

Ingredients
675 g (1-1/2 lb) small zucchini, unpeeled
90 mL (6 tablespoons) olive oil
1 clove garlic, crushed
1 large onion, chopped
30 mL (2 tablespoons) tomato paste
125 mL (1/2 cup) white wine
2 mL (1/2 teaspoon) thyme
1 bay leaf
12 grains coriander
12 peppercorns
250 mL (1 cup) water
30 mL (2 tablespoons) olive oil
30 mL (2 tablespoons) lemon juice
30 mL (2 tablespoons) fresh parsley, chopped

Method
— Put the 90 mL (6 tablespoons) of oil, garlic and onion in a dish; cook at 100% for 2 to 3 minutes, stirring once during the cooking time.
— Add the tomato paste, wine, seasonings and water and mix well.
— Cook at 100% for 7 minutes, stirring once during the cooking time.
— In the meantime, cut off the ends of the zucchini, cut into 4 strips lengthwise and then cut into 5 cm (2 in) lengths.
— Add to the liquid and stir.
— Cover and cook at 100% for 9 to 11 minutes, stirring once during the cooking time.
— Let cool and refrigerate.
— Marinate for 2 hours.
— Remove the bay leaf; add the 30 mL (2 tablespoons) of oil and lemon juice and stir.
— Garnish with parsley before serving.

The originality of this simple recipe, made with ordinary ingredients, will surprise your guests.

Cut the zucchini into 4 strips, lengthwise, and then into 5 cm (2 in) lengths.

After marinating the cooked zucchini, remove the bay leaf and add the oil and lemon juice.

Egg and Lemon Soup (Greece)

Level of Difficulty	
Preparation Time	20 min
Cost per Serving	$
Number of Servings	8
Nutritional Value	70 calories 3.9 g protein 8.6 g carbohydrate
Food Exchanges	0.5 oz meat 1-1/2 vegetable exchanges
Cooking Time	2 h 20 min
Standing Time	None
Power Level	100%, 90%
Write Your Cooking Time Here	

Ingredients
125 mL (1/2 cup) long grain rice
3 egg yolks
juice of 2 lemons

Bouillon:
1 chicken carcass
2 carrots, finely sliced
1 onion, finely sliced
2 stalks celery, finely sliced
15 mL (1 tablespoon) parsley, chopped
5 mL (1 teaspoon) thyme
1 bay leaf
salt and pepper to taste
2 L (8 cups) water

Method
— In a large dish, combine all the bouillon ingredients and stir.
— Cover and cook at 100% for 30 minutes.
— Skim the foam from the surface of the bouillon and continue to cook at 90% for 1-1/2 hours, skimming twice during the cooking time.
— Strain the bouillon and remove the particles of fat suspended on the surface.
— Add the rice to the bouillon, cover and cook at 100% for 15 to 18 minutes or until the rice is cooked.
— Whisk the egg yolks with the lemon juice until the mixture is pale and foamy.
— While whisking, slowly add 50 mL (1/4 cup) of the bouillon.
— Blend the egg mixture into the bouillon, whisking continuously.
— Cook at 100% for 2 minutes; do not allow the soup to boil.

This succulent recipe will please everyone at the table. First assemble these ingredients.

In a large dish, combine all the bouillon ingredients and stir. Cover and cook at 100% for 30 minutes.

Strain the bouillon and remove the fat particles from the surface.

Germany:
From One Abundant Plate to Another

To those who know German food only by reputation, a typical meal from Germany would include a variety of sausages, cabbage and potatoes—all washed down, naturally, by a tall stein of beer and finished off with a pastry for dessert!

Obviously this caricature does have a grain of truth. The famous German festivals such as the Oktoberfest in Munich—16 days of parties during which millions of liters of beer and kilos of sausage are wolfed down to the prominent sound of Bavarian orchestras—contribute to this reputation. Village fairs, numerous throughout the summer months, are good excuses to sample the many varieties (more than 100) of famous sausages, such as *Bierwurst, Leberwurst* and *Weisswurst,* served hot or cold with sharp mustard.

That Germans have a predilection for their sausages is altogether true and, indeed, their popularity has spread throughout the world. The famous sausage from Frankfurt, the frankfurter, served in a bun with mustard, is the ancestor of our hot dog.

The old vision of stocky, round-faced Germans seated at tables around a bottle of good Riesling and a plate of sauerkraut is one that is fast fading. But Germans are still well known for their hospitality and they hold it so dearly that there is a special word for it in the German language, one that cannot be translated precisely: *Gemütlichkeit.* *Gemütlichkeit* describes the feeling of comfort induced by get-togethers with friends at home or at the local pub— the *Weistube, Bierhall, Gästhof* or *Lokal*—when everyone feels at ease and welcome. The word describes an ambiance unique to German evenings.

As in all countries, in Germany special occasions call for special dishes. Among these specialties, we should mention *Schnitzel:* veal cutlets, sometimes breaded and served in a variety of ways. With a delicious cream sauce it is *Rahmschnitzel,* with a mushroom and sour cream sauce it becomes *Jägerschnitzel* and stuffed with ham and cheese we have *Käseschnitzel.* Spätzle, small dumplings made with a white flour dough (sometimes mixed with puréed spinach) and cooked in boiling water, are usually served with *Schnitzel* and are ideal for soaking up the creamy sauces. Spätzle are used instead of potatoes and can be made in several different ways.

A meal served with a white Rhine wine or a Moselle is still not complete unless it includes one of the very sweet Austrian desserts that Germans love so much, Black Forest cake (a cake with cherries) and *Sachertorte* being just two examples. The average German's timetable always leaves room for a break called *Kaffee-Trinken.* During the afternoon it is traditional for Germans to pause for a cup of coffee and a sweet—cookies, pastries, apple strudel or a piece of cream cake, as only they can make them.

Kirsch winds up an abundant supper and marks the beginning of cheerful conversation. The more intrepid guests will dedicate the evening to a game of *Kugelbahn* (a sort of German bowling) and celebrate victory with a round of schnapps, a liqueur made from potatoes.

Beef Roulades (Germany)

Level of Difficulty	🍴🍴 🍴🍴
Preparation Time	20 min
Cost per Serving	$
Number of Servings	8
Nutritional Value	266 calories 17.4 g protein 17.5 g lipids
Food Exchanges	2 oz meat 1 vegetable exchange 2 fat exchanges
Cooking Time	15 min
Standing Time	None
Power Level	100%, 70%
Write Your Cooking Time Here	

Ingredients
8 eye of the round beef fillets, 3 mm (1/8 in) thick
115 g (4 oz) bacon
1 onion, chopped
50 mL (1/4 cup) flour
5 mL (1 teaspoon) paprika
pepper to taste
45 mL (3 tablespoons) oil
1 carrot, finely sliced
1 stalk celery, finely sliced
1 leek, white part only, finely sliced
30 mL (2 tablespoons) parsley, chopped
250 mL (1 cup) beef bouillon
15 mL (1 tablespoon) cornstarch
30 mL (2 tablespoons) cold water

Method
— Put the bacon on a rack and cook at 100% for 3 to 4 minutes.
— Coarsely chop the bacon.
— Sprinkle an equal amount of onion and bacon on each of the fillets.
— Roll the fillets up and secure with toothpicks.
— Combine the flour, paprika and pepper.
— Dredge the roulades in the seasoned flour.
— Preheat a browning dish at 100% for 7 minutes; add the oil and heat at 100% for 30 seconds.
— Sear the roulades; add the vegetables and the parsley.
— Cover and cook at 70% for 4 to 6 minutes, or until done to your liking. Move the roulades from the center of the dish toward the outside halfway through the cooking time.
— Remove the roulades and set aside.
— Dissolve the cornstarch in the cold water, add it to the bouillon and cook at 100% for 3 to 5 minutes, stirring twice during the cooking time.
— Pour the sauce over the roulades before serving.

40

This typical German dish is as succulent as it is original and can be prepared in less than an hour. First assemble all the ingredients needed to make the dish.

Sprinkle the coarsely chopped cooked bacon and the onion evenly over each fillet of beef.

Roll up the fillets, secure with toothpicks and then dredge in the mixture of flour, paprika and pepper.

Poached Meatballs with Lemon Sauce (Germany)

Level of Difficulty	🍴
Preparation Time	20 min
Cost per Serving	$
Number of Servings	4
Nutritional Value	160 calories 27.9 g protein 4 mg iron
Food Exchanges	2.5 oz meat
Cooking Time	14 min
Standing Time	None
Power Level	100%, 90%
Write Your Cooking Time Here	

Ingredients
450 g (1 lb) ground beef
125 mL (1/2 cup) Italian breadcrumbs
1 egg
5 mL (1 teaspoon) lemon zest, grated
250 mL (1 cup) beef consommé
15 mL (1 tablespoon) cornstarch
45 mL (3 tablespoons) cold water
15 mL (1 tablespoon) lemon juice
1 egg yolk
salt and pepper to taste
5 mL (1 teaspoon) dried parsley

Method
— In a bowl, combine the ground beef, breadcrumbs, egg and lemon zest; mix until smooth.
— Form 12 meatballs of uniform size and set aside.
— Heat the consommé at 100% for 3 to 4 minutes or until boiling.
— Put the meatballs into the hot consommé and poach at 90% for 6 to 8 minutes, stirring once during the cooking time.
— Remove the meatballs an cover them with aluminum foil; set aside.
— Dissolve the cornstarch in the water and add it to the bouillon; add the lemon juice and stir.
— Cook at 100% for 1 to 2 minutes, stirring twice during the cooking time.
— Beat the egg yolk, add a little of the sauce and mix well. Blend the egg yolk into the sauce.
— Season to taste and add the parsley.
— Pour the sauce over the meatballs before serving.

This unpretentious recipe is an interesting variation on traditional ground beef dishes. First assemble the required ingredients.

Form 12 uniform meatballs with the mixture of ground beef, breadcrumbs, egg and lemon zest.

Remove the poached meatballs, cover them with aluminum foil and set aside.

Eastern Europe: A Cuisine without Borders

The countries of Eastern Europe have had a turbulent political history. The cultural influences of conquering countries and, more recently, of neighboring countries, have affected the different culinary traditions of these countries which, while exhibiting many common features, nevertheless remain amazingly diverse.

Rumanian, Polish, Hungarian, Czechoslovakian and Russian cooking are characterized by their abundance and substance. Everyday cooking is usually simple, but this simplicity is compensated for by the wide variety of dishes. Important ingredients include cabbage, prepared in many different ways, potatoes and lamb meat, which provide a vast array of delicatessen cuts. Soup is an essential part of every meal, as is bread, usually black, and spirits such as the famous vodka. Cooking is often highly seasoned and accompanied by sour or sweet and sour sauces and such spiced condiments as horseradish. One of the best-known soups of Eastern Europe is the hearty Hungarian *gulyás,* which owes its characteristic flavor to paprika, a spice basic to cooking throughout this country. Hungarian cooking is also known for its use of pork, onions, sour cream and freshwater fish.

The countries of Eastern Europe were strongly influenced by Scandinavia and this is the origin of their smoked meats and fish as well as their marinated, flavored vegetables such as pickles and cucumbers. The USSR has maintained the opulent Scandinavian buffet known as the smörgasbord, made up of small hot and cold dishes, called *zavouski* in the Soviet Union.

In the southern and eastern parts of the USSR the oriental influence is felt. The cuisine is somewhat less spicy and lamb is used more often, although beef and veal are still widely consumed.

Because of its demographic variety and its sheer size, the Soviet Union—the largest country in the world with 110 ethnic groups spread over two continents—is the country which has felt the most foreign influences. Its own culture, and thus its cuisine, is a veritable mosaic. In fact, sauerkraut (cabbage fermented in brine) comes from the USSR, which adapted this Chinese recipe acquired during the invasion of the Mongols in the thirteenth century.

As a result of the privations which have long beset its people, traditional Russian cooking is simple, hearty and healthy. Bread and soup, prepared in a multitude of ways, are basic foods. The best known are borsch (beet soup) and Russian cabbage soup, which any visitor to the Soviet Union will frequently find on the menu.

Russian cooking has been considerably influenced by French cuisine. Some of the best-known Russian dishes, such as Beef Stroganoff and Charlotte Russe, were in fact created by French chefs for francophile csars who reigned until the 1917 revolution.

The astonishing diversity in Eastern European and Russian cooking is a pleasure to discover. Na zdorovie! (To Your Health!)

Hunter's Stew (Poland)

Level of Difficulty	🍴🍴
Preparation Time	40 min*
Cost per Serving	$ $
Number of Servings	8
Nutritional Value	476 calories 30.2 g protein 24.9 g lipids
Food Exchanges	4 oz meat 1 fruit exchange 2 vegetable exchanges 1-1/2 fat exchanges
Cooking Time	53 min
Standing Time	5 min
Power Level	90%, 100%, 70%
Write Your Cooking Time Here	

* Soak the mushrooms in water for 12 hours before cooking.

Ingredients
30 g (1 oz) dried mushrooms
340 g (12 oz) Polish sausage
115 g (4 oz) uncooked ham
250 mL (1 cup) hot water
400 g (14 oz) cabbage, chopped
2 large potatoes, chopped
30 mL (2 tablespoons) butter
2 onions, chopped
900 g (2 lb) sauerkraut
340 g (12 oz) beef or veal roast, cooked and cut into cubes
225 g (8 oz) rabbit meat, cooked and cut into cubes
20 prunes, pitted and sliced
15 mL (1 tablespoon) sugar
250 mL (1 cup) red wine

Method
— Put the mushrooms in a bowl and cover them with water.
— Soak for 12 hours.
— Remove the mushrooms, drain and cut them into thin slices; set the mushrooms and the liquid aside.
— Put the sausages and ham into a casserole and add the hot water.
— Cook at 90% for 15 minutes, stirring halfway through the cooking time.
— Remove the meat and add the cabbage and potatoes to the liquid.
— Cover and cook at 100% for 8 to 10 minutes, stirring once during the cooking time.
— Drain and set aside.
— Cut the sausages into 2.5 cm (1 in) pieces and cut the ham into cubes; set aside.
— Put the mushrooms, butter and onion in a dish; cover and cook at 100% for 2 to 3 minutes, stirring once during cooking, and set aside.

— Drain the sauerkraut.
— In a large casserole, combine the remaining ingredients, except the wine with all the ingredients that have been set aside (including the mushroom liquid).
— Cover and cook at 70% for 10 minutes; stir.
— Add the wine, cover and cook at 70% for 10 to 15 minutes, stirring once during the cooking time.
— Let stand for 5 minutes and serve.

MICROTIPS

What Is Sauerkraut?

Sauerkraut is a German word literally meaning sour cabbage. It is chopped white cabbage salted and fermented in brine. Sauerkraut is served hot and is often accompanied by boiled potatoes and small pieces of salt pork, ham, frankfurters or other types of sausage. Canned sauerkraut can be found in most supermarkets; some specialty grocery stores also sell it fresh.

Cabbage Rolls (Russia)

Level of Difficulty	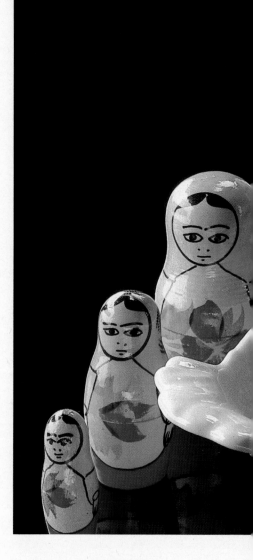
Preparation Time	30 min
Cost per Serving	$
Number of Servings	6
Nutritional Value	322 calories 30.9 g protein 4.2 mg iron
Food Exchanges	3.5 oz meat 3 vegetable exchanges
Cooking Time	30 min
Standing Time	5 min
Power Level	100%, 70%
Write Your Cooking Time Here	

Ingredients
1 white cabbage
225 g (8 oz) lean ground beef
225 g (8 oz) lean ground pork
225 g (8 oz) lean ground veal
50 mL (1/4 cup) instant rice
1 egg
salt and pepper to taste
750 mL (3 cups) boiling water
125 mL (1/2 cup) water
1 540 mL (19 oz) can tomato sauce
1 onion, chopped

Method
— In a bowl, combine the ground meats, rice and egg; season and mix; set aside.
— Remove 12 cabbage leaves, put them in a large bowl and cover with the boiling water.
— Cook at 100% for 4 to 5 minutes.
— Drain and dry the cabbage leaves and spread 15 mL (1 tablespoon) of the meat filling over each.
— Roll up the cabbage leaves and secure with toothpicks.
— Combine the 125 mL (1/2 cup) water and the tomato paste and mix well.
— Chop the remaining cabbage leaves and put into a casserole with the onion.
— Place the stuffed cabbage rolls on top and pour the tomato sauce over them.
— Cover and cook at 70% for 20 to 25 minutes, moving the cabbage rolls from the center of the casserole to the outside halfway through the cooking time.
— Let stand for 5 minutes and serve.

These are the ingredients you will need to prepare this recipe, suitable for any occasion.

Cook the cabbage leaves in boiling water.

Halfway through the cooking time, move the stuffed cabbage rolls from the center of the casserole toward the outside to ensure uniform cooking.

Red Mullet with Lemon and Chives (Rumania)

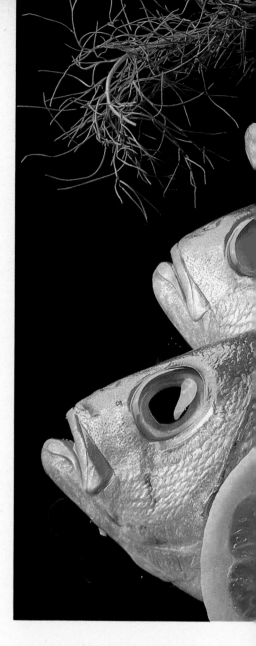

Level of Difficulty	🍴
Preparation Time	15 min
Cost per Serving	$
Number of Servings	4
Nutritional Value	270 calories 45.3 g protein 7.6 g lipids
Food Exchanges	5 oz meat 1 fat exchange
Cooking Time	18 min
Standing Time	5 min
Power Level	70%
Write Your Cooking Time Here	

Ingredients
4 whole red mullets
pepper to taste
8 thin lemon slices
30 mL (2 tablespoons) chives, chopped
15 mL (1 tablespoon) parsley, chopped
30 mL (2 tablespoons) butter

Method
— Clean and scale the fish; pepper the cavities.
— Score the surface of the fish with a knife.
— Put the fish in a large dish and place the lemon slices, chives and parsley on top.
— Put an equal amount of the butter on each fish.
— Cover and cook at 70% for 8 minutes.
— Move the fish from the center of the dish to the outside.
— Cover the dish again and continue cooking at 70% for 8 to 10 minutes or until the fish is cooked.
— Let stand for 5 minutes and serve.

All your guests will enjoy this delicious dish. First assemble the ingredients required.

Score the surface of each fish with a knife.

Place the lemon slices, chives, parsley and butter on the fish before cooking.

England: Savory and Simple

English cooking is proof that traditions can be handed down from generation to generation for centuries. Perhaps because of the insularity of the United Kingdom, its cuisine has maintained the simplicity of robust and savory medieval cooking. Often ignored, even slighted, English cuisine deserves to be better known and appreciated. For, in fact, whoever conquers his prejudices and samples English dishes will discover with pleasure a more varied cuisine than expected, one made up of many regional dishes.

Fish has an important place in English cuisine; both saltwater and freshwater fish are prepared in many different ways. The most famous fish dish is certainly fish and chips, which all tourists to the land of Albion have to try. The lightly salted and smoked herring, called kipper, is a classic English dish as well and the recipe for Smoked Haddock, on page 56, is another.

The British are big beef and lamb eaters and they prepare excellent stews; every region has its own special recipe. Fruits and cereals are included in many dishes. And, as we know, savory pies of all types play a very important role in English cuisine, beef and kidney pie being one of England's most famous dishes. These abundant dishes are just right for long rainy days, when the dampness can chill even the hardiest soul!

Great Britain's colonial past explains the presence of curries and chutneys in the diet of the English. These typically Indian recipes have been adapted over time to English tastes.

Finally, England is a country with strongly rooted traditions, its cuisine reflecting ties with its past, especially during the celebration of annual holidays. The Christmas turkey and plum pudding have become ritual dishes in a number of other countries as well. Desserts made with dried or candied fruits (Corinth raisins, candied fruit rind, dried apricots) are very much a part of British cooking.

This solid cuisine is often served with a light or dark beer, and best enjoyed at the local pub!

Plum Pudding (England)

Level of Difficulty	🍴🍴
Preparation Time	30 min
Cost per Serving	$ $ $
Number of Servings	20
Nutritional Value	273 calories 36.8 g carbohydrate
Food Exchanges	2 fruit exchanges 1 bread exchange 1 fat exchange
Cooking Time	14 min
Standing Time	15 min
Power Level	100%, 50%
Write Your Cooking Time Here	

Ingredients
125 mL (1/2 cup) dried raisins, soaked in water
125 mL (1/2 cup) molasses
175 mL (3/4 cup) brown sugar
10 mL (2 teaspoons) baking soda
250 mL (1 cup) candied fruit, chopped
90 mL (3 oz) rum
0.5 mL (1/8 teaspoon) nutmeg
pinch cinnamon
1 mL (1/4 teaspoon) salt
zest of half a lemon and half an orange
2 eggs
2 egg yolks

250 mL (1 cup) lamb suet, chopped
375 mL (1-1/2 cups) flour
250 mL (1 cup) breadcrumbs
175 mL (3/4 cup) milk

Icing (if desired):
125 mL (1/2 cup) fruit jelly
icing sugar to taste
125 mL (1/2 cup) cognac

Method
— Drain the raisins and set aside.
— Combine the molasses, brown sugar and baking soda; add the candied fruit, raisins, rum, nutmeg, cinnamon, salt and zests and mix well.
— Blend in the eggs, egg yolks and suet; set aside.
— In another bowl, combine the flour, breadcrumbs and milk; blend into the first mixture in three parts, mixing constantly to obtain a smooth consistency.
— Pour the batter into a tube pan.
— Place the pan on a raised rack in the oven and cook at 50% for 6 minutes. Give the dish a half-turn and continue cooking for 6 minutes or

until the pudding is cooked.
— Let stand for 10 to 15 minutes.
— Unmold by inverting the pudding onto a plate.
— To prepare the icing, first heat the fruit jelly at 100% for 45 seconds.
— Brush the jelly over the pudding and sprinkle with icing sugar.
— Heat the cognac at 100% for 40 seconds; pour the cognac over the pudding and flambé.

MICROTIPS

Plum Pudding: A Quintessential British Tradition

Like all other traditional dishes, plum pudding can be made in many different ways. The recipe opposite contains lamb suet. It can be replaced by suet from veal or beef kidneys, which will give the pudding a less pronounced taste. The icing suggested here can also be replaced by a simple cognac and butter sauce.

Smoked Haddock (England)

Level of Difficulty	🍴
Preparation Time	30 min
Cost per Serving	$ $
Number of Servings	4
Nutritional Value	481 calories 31.7 g protein 217.2 mg calcium
Food Exchanges	3 oz meat 2 bread exchanges 1/2 milk exchange 1 vegetable exchange 2-1/2 fat exchanges
Cooking Time	17 min
Standing Time	None
Power Level	100%, 70%
Write Your Cooking Time Here	

Ingredients

450 g (1 lb) smoked haddock fillets
500 mL (2 cups) milk
pepper to taste
4 large tomatoes
750 mL (3 cups) boiling water
225 g (8 oz) mushrooms, finely chopped
50 mL (1/4 cup) butter
50 mL (1/4 cup) flour
675 g (1-1/2 lb) potatoes, mashed

Method

— Put the haddock in a dish and add the milk; add pepper to taste and set aside.
— Blanch the tomatoes in the boiling water; peel, seed and chop them coarsely.
— Add the mushrooms and mix well.
— Pour the mixture over the fish fillets and dot with a small amount of the butter.
— Cover and cook at 100% for 5 minutes.
— Reduce the power to 70% and continue to cook for 4 to 6 minutes, giving the dish a half-turn halfway through the cooking time.
— Carefully transfer the fish to a serving platter. Set the cooking liquid aside.
— In another dish, melt the remaining butter at 100% for 30 seconds, add the flour and mix well.
— Blend the roux into the cooking liquid, mixing well, and cook at 100% for 2 to 3 minutes, stirring twice during the cooking time.
— Place the prepared mashed potatoes on the serving platter around the fish. Spoon some of the sauce over the fish and heat through at 100% for 1 to 2 minutes.
— Pour the rest of the sauce into a sauce boat before serving.

First assemble all the ingredients needed to prepare this dish, which is bound to be a big success with haddock lovers.

Blanch the tomatoes to make peeling them easier.

Pour the mixture of chopped tomatoes and mushrooms over the fish fillets before cooking.

The Middle East: A Subtle Mosaic of Flavors

The Middle East (or Near East) is a vast region which includes Israel, Egypt, Lebanon, Syria, Jordan, Iraq and the countries of the Arabian peninsula. The Middle East has for a long time been one of the crossroads of international commerce and its cuisine is inspired equally by the culinary traditons of Europe, the Far East and the Arab countries. Middle Eastern cuisine does however have certain characteristics common to every country there.

First of all rice is frequently used in its dishes as are typically Mediterranean vegetables such as eggplant, tomato, onion and peppers. Lamb and mutton are also widely consumed. Finally, Middle Easterners have developed fabulous sweet pastry recipes for desserts. The best known is baklava, a very sweet triangular pastry made with fine flaky egg dough, filled with grilled almonds and pistachios and covered in honey or rosewater syrup. For everyday, however, dessert is usually a platter of candied or dried dated, or simply a bowl of fresh dates served with a bowl of milk.

In the next few pages we will take a closer look at the cuisines of Lebanon and Egypt. There, as in all Arab countries, dried legumes, especially lentils and chick peas, are important ingredients. In Lebanon they are used to garnish couscous, a dish made with semolina grains and various vegetables and meat.

But the most impressive aspect of Lebanese cuisine is its hors d'oeuvres: sheep's tongue or cubed kidney served in a vinaigrette sauce, spinach or ground meat puff pastries, beans in a warm salad or puréed and sautéed in sesame oil, eggplant or chick pea purée, cucumbers in mint and yoghurt, stuffed vine leaves and so on.

Lebanese cuisine also offers a wide variety of main courses. In the West, we tend to think of kebabs as typical of Lebanese cooking: skewers of marinated cubed meat, usually lamb, grilled or roasted. Ground lamb meatballs, served with bulgur (cracked wheat grains), onions, parsley, pine nuts or almonds, are skewered and cook on the grill. Just as popular is couscous with saffron-flavored chicken rather than vegetables. A dish of lamb cut into strips and grilled on skewers, served with a rice salad, also frequents the family table.

Another popular dish is tabboulé. A refreshing chilled salad made with bulgur, tomatoes, mint, parsley and aromatics and dressed with a lemon vinaigrette, tabboulé is found on more and more North American restaurant menus.

Egyptian cooking has lost much of the ostentation which once characterized the feasts of the pharaohs. However, a whole lamb or goat cooked on an open-air grill is still the uncontested highlight of holiday meals. Like everywhere else in the Middle East, fresh herbs and spices flavor all dishes. *Molokheya,* a special soup made with a thick, spicy herbal bouillon and garnished with strips of chicken is a perfect example, as is our recipe for Grilled Fish with Coriander on page 60.

Grilled Fish with Coriander (Egypt)

Level of Difficulty	🍴🍴
Preparation Time	10 min*
Cost per Serving	**$**
Number of Servings	4
Nutritional Value	154 calories 18.3 g protein 8 g lipids
Food Exchanges	3 oz meat
Cooking Time	7 min
Standing Time	2 min
Power Level	70%
Write Your Cooking Time Here	✏️🍎

*Marinate the fish for 1 hour before cooking.

Ingredients
4 white fish fillets of your choice
salt and pepper to taste
1 small bouquet of fresh coriander; chopped

Marinade:
75 mL (5 tablespoons) olive oil
lemon juice
3 cloves garlic, crushed

Method
— In a bowl, combine all the marinade ingredients and sprinkle over the fish fillets.
— Marinate the fish for 1 hour.
— Drain the fish.
— Put the fish on a rack in a dish, placing the fleshy parts toward the outside of the dish; salt and pepper to taste.
— Cook at 70% for 5 to 7 minutes, giving the dish a half-turn halfway through the cooking time.
— Sprinkle with the fresh coriander.
— Cover and let stand for 2 minutes.

Assemble only these few ingredients to prepare these delicious fish fillets in less than half an hour.

Marinate the fish for 1 hour before cooking.

Put the fish on a rack in a dish, placing the fleshy parts of the fish toward the outside.

Meat Loaf with Pistachios (Lebanon)

Level of Difficulty	🍴🍴
Preparation Time	15 min*
Cost per Serving	$ $
Number of Servings	8
Nutritional Value	298 calories 32.4 g protein 14.9 g lipids
Food Exchanges	4 oz meat
Cooking Time	19 min
Standing Time	None
Power Level	100%, 70%
Write Your Cooking Time Here	

* Let the meat loaf cool before serving.

Ingredients
900 g (2 lb) lean ground beef
1 egg white
salt and pepper to taste
cinnamon to taste
250 mL (1 cup) chopped pistachios
250 mL (1 cup) red wine

Method
— Blend the egg white into the meat.
— Season with salt, pepper and cinnamon and mix well.
— Shape the meat into a rectangle on a chopping board.
— Sprinkle the chopped pistachios evenly over the meat.
— Roll up the meat, jelly roll fashion, and place it in a rectangular baking dish.
— Cook at 100% for 8 minutes, giving the dish a half-turn halfway through the cooking time.
— Continue cooking at 70% for 6 minutes.
— Pour the wine over the meat and give the dish a half-turn.
— Continue cooking at 70% for 4 to 5 minutes.
— Let cool and slice before serving.

This unique recipe will bring you many compliments. First assemble these ingredients.

Shape the meat into a rectangle and sprinkle with chopped pistachios.

Roll up the meat and place in a rectangular baking dish before cooking.

The Far East: Refinement and Subtlety

Any mention of oriental cooking has to start with rice. A basic food for billions of people, rice is even served for breakfast in the East. Rice is both a reward after work and a source of labor: the emblem of a whole section of humanity, industrious and organized. But rice rewards mainly those who cultivate it; it is a very nutritious food, containing protein, vitamins and minerals.

Unfortunately, modern processing methods cause rice to lose much of its nutritional value. Natural rice is rich in starch; for this reason oriental cooking requires that rice be thoroughly rinsed (to remove the layer of starch) before it is plunged into boiling water.

The cultivation of rice is ancient. Over the centuries, the Chinese have cultivated several different varieties of rice; as well as the famous white rice, there is brown, yellow, red and even green rice. And the different methods of preparing and serving rice are innumerable.

Oriental cooking can be extremely elaborate. For example, Peking duck takes three days to cook if traditonal methods are used. The microwave oven is particularly suited to this cuisine because it provides us with an opportunity to attempt the dishes preparation of which would otherwise try the patience of a saint. A number of oriental recipes have been successfully adapted to the microwave oven, including egg foo-yong, chop suey and snow peas.

Chinese vegetables are readily available in our grocery stores; green peppers, bean sprouts, snow peas, Chinese lettuce and Chinese cabbage *(bok-choi)* can be bought fresh in almost any supermarket. Less common products, such as water chestnuts and bamboo shoots, are sold in cans. Finally, you can discover a whole range of oriental products, such as dehydrated mushrooms and dried shrimps, by strolling through Chinatown.

As far as seasonings are concerned, soy sauce is the prime ingredient. Another sauce used in cooking is hoisin, a brown sauce made with soy sauce, sugar, water, spices, garlic and chili paste. Oyster sauce, a brown sauce made with oysters, hoisin and brine, contributes to the flavor of a number of special dishes. We should also mention sesame oil, a fat that is used in small quantities—not for frying but for enhancing the flavor of soups and vegetables.

Chinese desserts are healthy and frugal; sweet fruits such as lichees, mangoes or kumquats, in their own syrup, are served instead of rich heavy pastries.

To sit down at a Far Eastern table is to be surrounded by forty centuries of history, to discover an incredibly rich land and foods that are little known to Westerners and to share the cuisine of more than 25 percent of humanity. In a word, it is delightful.

Pork with Water Chestnuts (China)

Level of Difficulty	![fork and knife icon]
Preparation Time	20 min
Cost per Serving	$ $
Number of Servings	4
Nutritional Value	485 calories 20.2 g protein 4 mg iron
Food Exchanges	3 oz meat 2 vegetable exchanges 4-1/2 fat exchanges
Cooking Time	1 h
Standing Time	5 min
Power Level	100%, 50%
Write Your Cooking Time Here	

Ingredients
450 g (1 lb) pork loin, with rind
1 170 mL (6 oz) can water chestnuts
125 mL (1/2 cup) chicken bouillon
45 mL (3 tablespoons) soy sauce
30 mL (2 tablespoons) sugar
2 to 3 drops red food coloring
45 mL (3 tablespoons) oil
50 mL (1/4 cup) sherry

Method
— Cut the meat into 3.7 cm (1-1/2 in) cubes.
— Drain the water chestnuts; set aside.
— Combine the bouillon, soy sauce, sugar and food coloring; set aside.
— Preheat a browning dish at 100% for 7 minutes; add the oil and heat at 100% for 30 seconds.
— Sear the cubes of meat and the water chestnuts, then add the bouillon mixture.
— Cover and cook at 50% for 30 minutes, stirring once during the cooking time.
— Add the sherry and stir.
— Cover and cook at 50% for 25 to 30 minutes or until the pork is tender, stirring several times during the cooking.
— Let stand for 5 minutes.

This Chinese-style recipe will add an exotic note to your menu. These are the ingredients required.

Pour the mixture of chicken bouillon, soy sauce, sugar and food coloring over the pork and water chestnuts.

Add the sherry and stir before the final stage of cooking.

Short Ribs Korean Style

Level of Difficulty	🍴
Preparation Time	10 min
Cost per Serving	$
Number of Servings	4
Nutritional Value	255 calories 31.7 g protein 2.6 mg iron
Food Exchanges	3.5 oz meat
Cooking Time	1 h 5 min
Standing Time	None
Power Level	100%
Write Your Cooking Time Here	

Ingredients
1.6 kg (3-1/2 lb) short ribs of beef
2 cloves garlic, finely sliced
12 mushrooms, finely sliced
2 green onions, cut into
2.5 cm (1 in) lengths
5 mL (1 teaspoon) sesame seeds
5 mL (1 teaspoon) sesame oil
15 mL (1 tablespoon) sugar
salt and pepper to taste
15 mL (1 tablespoon) soy sauce

Method
— Put the short ribs into a casserole and cover with water.
— Cover and cook at 100% for 50 to 60 minutes or until the meat is tender, skimming off the fat several times.
— Add all the other ingredients and mix well.
— Cook at 100% for 5 minutes.
— Drain the meat and serve. Serve the bouillon in a separate bowl.

This exquisite dish can be prepared for cooking in a jiffy. First assemble these ingredients.

Cover the short ribs with water and cook at 100% for 50 to 60 minutes.

Skim the fat off several times during the cooking.

Add all the other ingredients before the final stage of cooking.

Chicken with Carrots in Sesame Sauce (Japan)

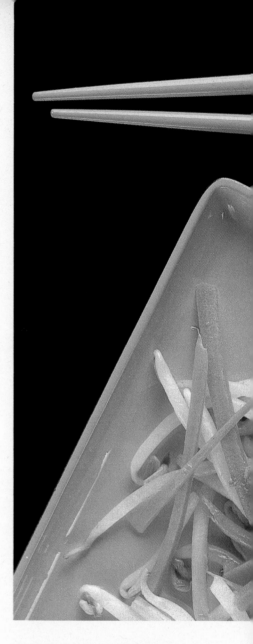

Level of Difficulty	⑪
Preparation Time	20 min*
Cost per Serving	$ $
Number of Servings	4
Nutritional Value	280 calories 31.2 g protein 2.5 mg iron
Food Exchanges	3 oz meat 2 vegetable exchanges 1/2 fat exchange
Cooking Time	20 min
Standing Time	None
Power Level	100%
Write Your Cooking Time Here	

*Marinate the chicken for 5 minutes before cooking.

Ingredients
450 g (1 lb) chicken, white meat only
30 mL (2 tablespoons) sake
2 carrots
45 mL (3 tablespoons) hot water
225 g (1/2 lb) soybean sprouts

Sauce:
15 mL (1 tablespoon) butter
30 mL (2 tablespoons) sesame seeds
30 mL (2 tablespoons) rice vinegar
30 mL (2 tablespoons) soy sauce
30 mL (2 tablespoons) sugar
15 mL (1 tablespoon) salt

Method
— Pierce the chicken in several places with a fork.
— Sprinkle with sake and marinate for 5 minutes.
— Cut the carrots into julienne strips and put them in a dish.
— Add the water, cover and cook at 100% for 3 to 4 minutes, stirring once during the cooking time.
— Drain the carrots and set aside.
— Rinse the soybean sprouts and put them in a dish; cover and cook at 100% for 2 to 3 minutes; drain and set them aside.
— Put the chicken in another dish and cover; cook at 100% for 7 to 9 minutes, stirring halfway through the cooking time.
— Cut the chicken into small cubes.
— Combine the chicken, carrots and bean sprouts; mix and set aside.
— To prepare the sauce, put the butter and the seasame seeds in a dish;

70

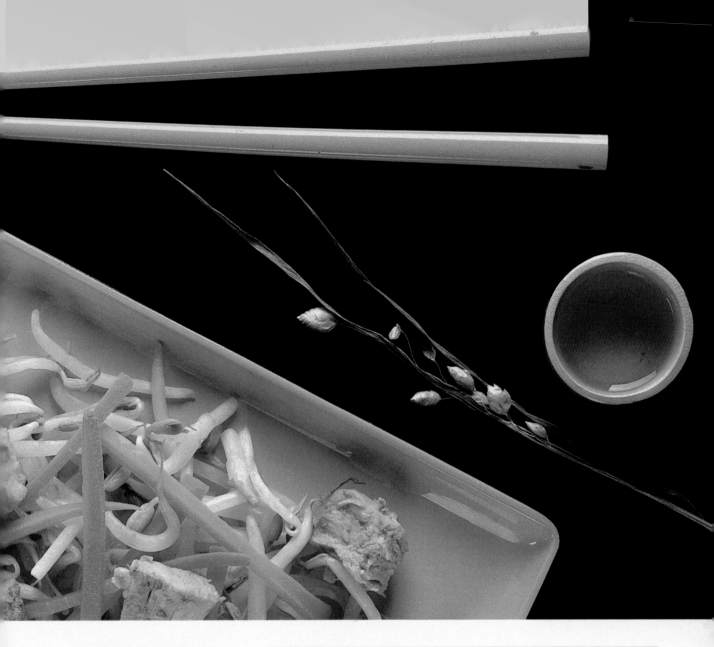

cook at 100% for 1 to 2
minutes or until the
sesame seeds are golden,
stirring once during the
cooking time.
— Crush the sesame seeds in
a mortar; add the
vinegar, soy sauce, sugar
and salt and stir until
smooth.
— Pour the sauce over the
chicken and vegetables
and heat through at
100% for 1 to 2 minutes
before serving.

MICROTIPS

**Cutting and
Chopping—Oriental
Style**

To master the art of
oriental-style cutting and
chopping, you must be
equipped with very
sharp utensils. Foods
sometimes need to be
cut into very thin slices,
strips or cubes, for
which a small cleaver is
normally used. If you
don't have one, use a
knife with a wide blade,
which also allows for
the cutting of the
thicker pieces of meat.

Spicy Beef Soup (Indonesia)

Level of Difficulty	🍴🍴
Preparation Time	20 min
Cost per Serving	**$**
Number of Servings	8
Nutritional Value	133 calories 16.2 g protein 2.2 mg iron
Food Exchanges	1.5 oz meat 1 fat exchange
Cooking Time	1 h 27 min
Standing Time	None
Power Level	100%
Write Your Cooking Time Here	

Ingredients
450 g (1 lb) beef brisket
salt to taste
115 g (4 oz) shrimp, cooked and shelled
6 green onions
3 cloves garlic
30 mL (2 tablespoons) oil
2 mL (1/2 teaspoon) ginger
pinch chili powder
2 mL (1/2 teaspoon) turmeric
10 mL (2 teaspoon) lemon juice

Method
— Put the beef in a dish and cover with salted water.
— Cover and cook at 100% for 1 hour, skimming the fat twice during the cooking.
— In the meantime, chop the shrimps, green onions and garlic; combine.
— Drain the beef and set both the beef and the bouillon aside.
— Pour the oil into a dish and heat at 100% for 1 minute; add the mixture of shrimp, green onion and garlic.
— Cover and cook at 100% for 2 minutes, stirring once during the cooking time.
— Add 250 mL (1 cup) of the bouillon, the ginger, chili powder and turmeric.
— Cover and cook at 100% for 15 minutes, stirring once during the cooking time.
— In the meantime, cut the meat into small cubes.

— Strain the shrimp mixture
  and retain only the liquid;
  add the remaining beef
  bouillon and the cubes of
  meat.
— Cover and cook at 100%
  for 7 to 9 minutes or
  until the soup is very hot.
— Add the lemon juice and
  serve immediately.

*These ingredients combine
beautifully to create an elegant
soup.*

*Strain the shrimp mixture and
retain only the liquid before
the final stage of cooking.*

Latin America: Colorful Cuisine

Latin America, lands of sun, high mountains and vast unexplored regions, offer simple, vigorous and colorful cuisine. In Mexico, Colombia, Argentina, Bolivia, Venezuela and Brazil, the sun's bounty produces a rich harvest of sweet, fragrant fruits as well as the fiery, passionate sun-filled chili, an essential ingredient in so many Latin American dishes. But on the other hand the omnipresent potatoes, beans and corn are symbolic of the aridity of a climate that allows only robust species to survive.

They say that corn is the wheat of Mexico and South America. However, corn flour does not contain the precious gluten that is essential to bread as we know it. Mexicans, therefore, make a sort of pancake called a tortilla, and there are as many different varieties of tortilla as there are rivers in the Andes!

For example, enchiladas garnished with fried sausages or roasted chicken are a more elaborate version of the tortilla. Mexicans also prepare tacos, tortillas that become soft when grilled. Tacos can be prepared with a filling or served dried as an appetizer to be dipped into a bean sauce. Nachos are yet another variation, covered with a spicy tomato sauce and garnished with cheese and sour cream.

The range of delicatessen items includes chorizos, lightly smoked sausages made with more or less spicy pork meat. In Peru fish is often prepared as a seviche, marinated raw fish garnished with red onions and served with sweet potatoes and corn. Lovers of exotic cuisine will be delighted to know that Brazilians eat hedgehog and that boiled monkey and alligator scallopini are very special dishes prepared by certain indigenous tribes. Of course, it is unlikely that these dishes will appear on our tables for some time to come!

South America is rich in tropical fruits: bananas, melons, oranges, lemons and coconuts grow abundantly as do pineapples, as large as footballs; guava, with their pulpy nectar; sweet-smelling mangoes; papayas, which has a special enzyme used to tenderize meat; and thirst-quenching grenadilla.

Vegetable cultivation is as abundant and diversified as that of fruit. In these countries there are varieties of potato, called *papa,* in the high mountains which can resist the night frost. Peppers, *jicamas* (a sort of turnip), cactus leaves and *aji* (from the chili family) are regulars on the daily menus of the people in this part of the world.

The avocado, which is really a fruit according to the strict botanical definition, is the basis of the famous *guacamole,* made with tomato and coriander. But chilis, those sharp little peppers, are the truly essential ingredients of this cuisine.

An exotic dish prepared with sweet potatoes or coconut is surely worth a trip, at least for a few minutes, to Peru or Venezuela.

Chicken with Chili Pepper and Tomato Sauce (Mexico)

Level of Difficulty	🍴
Preparation Time	20 min*
Cost per Serving	$
Number of Servings	6
Nutritional Value	310 calories 34.1 g protein 2.7 mg iron
Food Exchanges	3 oz meat 1 vegetable exchange 2 fat exchanges
Cooking Time	48 min
Standing Time	10 min
Power Level	100%, 70%
Write Your Cooking Time Here	

*Marinate the chili peppers in the hot chicken bouillon for 30 minutes.

Ingredients
1 1.8 kg (4 lb) chicken, cut into serving pieces
6 dried red chili peppers
250 mL (1 cup) chicken bouillon
2 onions, chopped
3 tomatoes, peeled and chopped
1 clove garlic, chopped
15 mL (1 tablespoon) vinegar
5 mL (1 teaspoon) sugar
2 mL (1/2 teaspoon) coriander
1 mL (1/4 teaspoon) cinnamon
1 mL (1/4 teaspoon) cloves
7 mL (1-1/2 teaspoons) salt
2 mL (1/2 teaspoon) pepper
60 mL (4 tablespoons) butter

Method
— Chop up the chili peppers and set aside.
— Heat the chicken bouillon at 100% for 3 minutes or until boiling.
— Add the chili peppers and leave to marinate for 30 minutes.
— Put the chili peppers and bouillon into a blender and blend for a few seconds until puréed; add all the other ingredients except the chicken and the butter.
— Blend until thick.
— Strain the resulting sauce through a fine sieve and set aside.
— Preheat a browning dish

at 100% for 7 minutes; add the butter and heat at 100% for 30 seconds.
— Sear the pieces of chicken.
— Pour the sauce over the chicken, turning to coat each piece.
— Cover and cook at 70% for 20 minutes.
— Move the pieces of chicken from the center of the dish toward the outside.
— Cover and continue cooking at 70% for 20 to 25 minutes or until the chicken is tender.
— Let stand for 10 minutes before serving.

To save time and fuss, assemble the ingredients required before beginning the recipe.

Pork and Potatoes with Fruit Sauce (Peru)

Level of Difficulty	🍴🍽️
Preparation Time	30 min*
Cost per Serving	$
Number of Servings	8
Nutritional Value	320 calories 26 g protein 3.6 mg iron
Food Exchanges	3 oz meat 1/2 bread exchange 1 fat exchange
Cooking Time	1 h 16 min
Standing Time	10 min
Power Level	100%, 50%
Write Your Cooking Time Here	

* Marinate the pork for 6 hours at room temperature or for 12 hours in the refrigerator before cooking.

Ingredients
900 g (2 lb) pork, cut into
2.5 cm (1 in) cubes
4 potatoes, sliced
10 mL (2 teaspoons) cumin
10 mL (2 teaspoons) garlic
5 mL (1 teaspoon) salt
2 mL (1/2 teaspoon) pepper
250 mL (1 cup) white vinegar
45 mL (3 tablespoons) oil
500 mL (2 cups) hot water
250 mL (1 cup) orange juice
50 mL (1/4 cup) lemon juice

Method
— In a mortar, crush the cumin, garlic, salt and pepper.
— Add to the vinegar and mix well.
— Add the cubes of meat and marinate, covered, for 6 hours at room temperature or for 12 hours in the refrigerator.
— Remove the cubes of meat and dry well; reserve the marinade.
— Preheat a browning dish at 100% for 7 minutes; add the oil and heat at 100% for 30 seconds.
— Sear the meat; add the marinade and the hot water.
— Cover and cook at 100% for 5 minutes and stir.
— Cover and continue to cook at 50% for 45 to 60 minutes or until the meat is tender, stirring twice during the cooking time.
— Add the fruit juices and the potatoes.
— Cover and cook at 100% for 9 to 11 minutes, stirring once during the cooking time.
— Let stand for 10 minutes and serve.

This Peruvian recipe is sure to bring you many compliments. Assemble these ingredients before beginning.

Marinate the cubes of meat, covered, for 6 hours at room temperature or for 12 hours in the refrigerator.

When the pork is cooked, add the orange juice, lemon juice and the potatoes before proceeding with the final cooking stage.

Rabbit with Coconut (Venezuela)

Level of Difficulty	🍴
Preparation Time	40 min
Cost per Serving	$ $
Number of Servings	6
Nutritional Value	235 calories 28.2 g protein
Food Exchanges	3 oz meat 1/2 fruit exchange
Cooking Time	57 min
Standing Time	10 min
Power Level	100%, 70%
Write Your Cooking Time Here	

Ingredients
1 1.3 kg (3 lb) rabbit, cut into 6 pieces
1 fresh coconut
15 mL (1 tablespoon) cornstarch dissolved in 30 mL (2 tablespoons) cold water
3 tomatoes
1 onion, chopped
salt and pepper to taste

Method
— With a nail and hammer, pierce 3 small holes in the dark, smooth part of the coconut to drain the milk; set the milk aside.
— Put the coconut on a plate and heat at 100% for 2 minutes or until warm.
— Put the coconut on a chopping board and break it in two with a hammer.
— Remove the brown shell and cut the meat into pices.
— Add enough water to the coconut milk to obtain 500 mL (2 cups) of liquid.
— Pour the liquid into a blender and add the coconut meat; blend until a smooth purée is obtained.
— Strain through a fine sieve and again add enough water to obtain 500 mL (2 cups) of liquid. Press the mixture firmly with a spoon and discard the pulp.
— Pour the liquid into a

dish, add the dissolved cornstarch and heat at 100% for 4 to 6 minutes, stirring every 2 minutes or until thickened.
— In the meantime, blanch the tomatoes.
— Rinse the tomatoes in cold water, peel and cut them in two; press to extract the juice and the seeds and chop finely.
— Blend the tomatoes and onion at medium speed for a few seconds and

add to the coconut sauce; season.
— Cook at 100% for 7 to 9 minutes, stirring once during the cooking time.
— Add the rabbit and coat it well with the sauce.
— Cover and cook at 100% for 15 minutes.
— Stir the pieces of rabbit.
— Continue cooking at 70% for 20 to 25 minutes or until the rabbit is tender.
— Let stand for 10 minutes.

MICROTIPS

Peeling Tomatoes Easily
Tomatoes can be easily peeled if they are first blanched in the microwave oven. To do so, pour enough water into a casserole to cover the tomatoes. Cover, bring to a boil, plunge the tomatoes in it for just a few seconds and then rinse under cold water before peeling.

Rabbit with Coconut

This unusual recipe will impress all your guests. Assemble all these ingredients before beginning.

With a nail and hammer, pierce 3 small holes into the dark, smooth part of the coconut to extract the milk.

Remove the brown shell and cut the meat into pieces.

After blending the coconut meat and liquid, strain the purée through a fine sieve.

Add enough water to obtain 500 mL (2 cups) of liquid.

Press the mixture firmly with a spoon and discard the pulp.

MICROTIPS

The Aroma Sets the Mood

The delicious aromas that emanate from the kitchen tend to sharpen appetites and put guests in a receptive mood. However, the cabbage used in casserole dishes sometimes leaves a persistent odor that some people find unpleasant. To overcome this problem, serve the casserole with home-baked bread, which you can prepare in a jiffy in the microwave—and the wonderful scent will bring back many happy childhood memories.

Chicken, Ham and Rice Soup (Brazil)

Ingredients
1 chicken, 1.3 kg (3 lb), cut into 8 pieces
115 g (4 oz) ham, cut into cubes
125 mL (1/2 cup) long grain rice
1 onion, cut in two
1 L (4 cups) chicken bouillon
500 mL (2 cups) hot water
6 tomatoes, peeled, seeded and chopped
3 carrots, diced
pepper to taste
15 mL (1 tablespoon) fresh parsley, chopped

Method
— In a large casserole, combine the chicken, onion, bouillon and hot water.
— Cover and cook at 100% for 30 minutes.
— Turn the pieces of chicken over and skim off the fat.
— Cover and continue cooking at 100% for 30 minutes.
— Remove the chicken and let cool.
— Strain the bouillon through a fine sieve; discard the onion.

— Degrease the bouillon and add the tomatoes, carrots, rice and pepper.
— Cover and cook at 100% for 30 minutes, stirring once during the cooking time.
— Bone the chicken pieces and cut the meat into strips or cubes.
— Add the chicken and the ham cubes to the soup and cook at 100% for 3 minutes.
— Add the parsley and let stand for 5 minutes before cooking.

Braised Tuna (Brazil)

Level of Difficulty	🍴
Preparation Time	20 min*
Cost per Serving	$ $
Number of Servings	8
Nutritional Value	425 calories 48.1 g protein 21.1 g lipids
Food Exchanges	4.5 oz meat 1 vegetable exchange 1 fat exchange
Cooking Time	13 min
Standing Time	5 min
Power Level	100%, 70%
Write Your Cooking Time Here	🍎✏️

* Marinate the tuna at room temperature for 1 hour before cooking.

Ingredients
8 tuna steaks, weighing about
1.5 kg (3-1/4 lb) total
1 dry red chili pepper
2 cloves garlic, very finely
chopped
15 mL (1 tablespoon) salt
500 mL (2 cups) water
1 red pepper, chopped
75 mL (1/3 cup) flour
50 mL (1/4 cup) oil
2 onions, coarsely chopped
5 mL (1 teaspoon) thyme
30 mL (2 tablespoons) capers
juice of 1 lemon

Method
— In a mortar, crush the
chili peppers, garlic and
salt.
— Put this mixture into a
large bowl with the water
and the chopped red
pepper to make the
marinade.
— Put the tuna into the
marinade, cover and
marinate for 1 hour at
room temperature.
— Drain the tuna steaks, dry
well and dust with the
flour. Reserve the
marinade.
— Preheat a browning dish
at 100% for 7 minutes.

— In the meantime, strain
the marinade and set the
crushed chili pepper and
chopped red pepper
aside. Reserve 125 mL
(1/2 cup) of the liquid.
— Pour the oil into the
preheated browning dish
and heat at 100% for 30
seconds.
— Sear 4 of the steaks and
put them in another dish.
— Reheat the browning dish
at 100% for 4 minutes
and sear the remaining 4
steaks. Remove them and
cut all the steaks into

large serving pieces.
— Put the onion into a large dish and cook at 100% for 3 minutes; add the thyme and the capers.
— Add the fish, the vegetables from the marinade, 125 mL (1/2 cup) of the marinade and the lemon juice.
— Cover and cook at 70% for 9 to 10 minutes, giving the dish a half-turn halfway through the cooking time.
— Let stand for 5 minutes and serve.

Assemble these ingredients to prepare this delicious recipe in less than 40 minutes.

Strain the marinade and set the vegetables and 125 mL (1/2 cup) of the liquid aside.

Scandinavia:
Robust Cooking for a Harsh Climate

The Scandinavian countries, Denmark, Sweden, Norway and Iceland share a lengthy common history. As a result of many political alliances, each country has influenced the others, but not so much as to make their cuisine uniform. Actually, the strongest influence on Scandinavian cuisine has been its harsh northern climate.

As a result of their isolation during their long and rigorous winters, Scandinavians have developed many methods of preserving foods and thus their smoked meats and fish all have very pronounced flavors. They are especially known for preparing herring in many different ways.

Although these Nordic countries must survive long difficult winters, they also enjoy the midnight sun in summer, which provides lovely long, light-filled evenings and offers an opportunity for sharing meals with friends—meals which, fueled with a cask of aquavit and kegs of beer, can last all night.

Compared with its neighbors, Denmark's climate is relatively mild and its fields are luxuriant. Its dairy industry produces an impressive array of cheeses which are major ingredients in many of its recipes. The strong tasting Danish blue cheese is certainly the best known of Denmark's cheeses.

Traditional Danish cooking is lightly spiced but rich in butter and cream. Pork, potatoes and cabbage are basic foods. With a good bottle of light beer, the meal is complete.

But the Danish triumph when it comes to the dessert tray. We all know the sweet-smelling Danish pastries, especially good when warm, but our North American versions look meager beside the sumptuous shelves of pastries in the beautiful city of Copenhagen!

Sweden—probably the best known, in terms of cooking, of the Scandinavian countries—also has the most diversified cuisine. In the past, tradition required that when dinners were held for a group each person would bring one part of the meal. This tradition has evolved and habits changed, but this type of buffet (the famous smörgasbord) has not lost its popularity and is still enjoyed at home or in the most elegant restaurants. The traditional smörgasbord includes a wide variety of foods prepared in individual portions: sumptuous open-faced sandwiches, colorful salads, a profusion of sauces, cold cuts and smoked foods as well as breads and crackers of all types. Those invited to this opulent buffet are welcome to serve themselves to their heart's content.

Swedish cooking, which uses lamb, pork and beef as often as it does fish, is simple and savory but very artistic and imaginative in its preparation. For example, the delicate Veal Rolls described in the recipe on page 90 are so appetizing that they will make you look like a real chef, even before your guests have tasted them.

Norwegian and Icelandic cuisines are both vigorous, with robust flavors; fish, often smoked, and lamb are most popular. A plate of Baltic herring, decorated with a hint of fresh chives and served with a pot of dill pickles makes a simple, hearty and delicious meal.

Based essentially on meat and fish, the cuisine of the Scandinavian countries is robust and filling, ideal for hearty appetites. Perfect after a sauna and an icy swim!

17

derrière lui, le grand voilier Wavertree met le cap sur le grand large. Peinture de John Stobart, 1895.

Herring Oslo Style (Norway)

Level of Difficulty	🍴🍴
Preparation Time	30 min
Cost per Serving	$
Number of Servings	4
Nutritional Value	282 calories 33.5 g protein 12.7 g lipids
Food Exchanges	3.5 oz meat 1 fat exchange
Cooking Time	7 min
Standing Time	None
Power Level	100%, 90%
Write Your Cooking Time Here	

Ingredients
900 g (2 lb) fresh herring or smelt
30 mL (2 tablespoons) chives, finely chopped
30 mL (2 tablespoons) onion, grated
50 mL (1/4 cup) breadcrumbs
15 mL (1 tablespoon) oil
30 mL (2 tablespoon) butter

Method
— Clean the fish and remove the dorsal fins.
— Combine the chives, onion and breadcrumbs and mix well.
— Coat the fish with this mixture.
— Preheat a browning dish at 100% for 7 minutes.
— Add the oil and butter and heat at 100% for 30 seconds.
— Sear the fish.
— Without covering, cook at 90% for 5 to 7 minutes, or until the fish are cooked giving the dish a half-turn after 3 minutes.

MICROTIPS

A Glass of Aquavit?

Made for over five centuries, aquavit is the traditional Scandinavian alcoholic beverage. This perfumed liquor, the product of distilled potatoes or grains, is fermented in barrels and flavored with caraway seeds or other aromatic substances such as dill or anise.

The Smörgasbord

The literal translation of the word smörgasbord is "the buttered bread table." Today's smörgasbords are a flavorful example of the abundance of good food found in the Nordic countries.

A true smörgasbord includes four main types of dishes, served in the following order. First, different types of herring, the Number 1 fish in Scandinavia, are served. Then, other types of fish or fish-based appetizers are eaten. These appetizers are followed by a selection of cold meats and, finally, the hot dishes are presented.

The choice of foods on the buffet table is vast: smoked salmon canapés, fish aspics, fried shrimps with sauce, lobster salad, crab or vegetables, all sorts of marinated foods (beets, onions, capers and pickles) and cold meats (including pork tongue and roast beef). As for hot dishes, the recipes on pages 88 and 90 are both suitable.

This feast is complete with the addition of some bread, rye for example, or thin, crispy crackers and a platter of cheese.

Veal Rolls (Sweden)

Level of Difficulty	🍴🍴
Preparation Time	15 min
Cost per Serving	$ $
Number of Servings	8
Nutritional Value	283 calories 20.7 g protein 21.1 g lipids
Food Exchanges	3 oz meat 1-1/2 fat exchanges
Cooking Time	16 min
Standing Time	None
Power Level	100%, 70%
Write Your Cooking Time Here	

Ingredients
8 veal escallops, 3 mm
(1/8 in) thick
8 slices of ham, 3 mm
(1/8 in) thick
60 mL (4 tablespoons) butter
125 mL (1/2 cup) white wine
225 g (8 oz) Gruyère cheese,
grated

Method
— Preheat a browning dish
  at 100% for 7 minutes.
— In the meantime, arrange
  the slices of ham on top
  of the veal escallops.
— Roll up the escallops and
  secure with toothpicks.
— Put the butter in the
  heated browning dish and
  heat at 100% for 30
  seconds.
— Sear the veal rolls.
— Add the wine.
— Cover and cook at 70%
  for 8 to 10 minutes,
  moving the rolls from the
  center of the dish toward

the outside halfway
through the cooking time.
— Remove the rolls and
  keep them warm.
— Add the Gruyère to the
  cooking juices and stir.
— Cook at 100% for 6
  minutes, or until the
  cheese is hot, stirring
  twice during the cooking
  time.
— Pour the sauce over the
  rolls before serving.

First assemble the ingredients that make up this delicious Swedish-style recipe.

Roll up the escallops and secure them with toothpicks.

Add the Gruyère to the cooking juices before proceeding to the final stage of cooking.

The United States: Melting Pot Cuisine

To give a brief overview of American cuisine would be impossible. With its 50 states, its varied climatic regions, its history of uninterrupted conquests and its two centuries of massive immigration, this country enjoys cuisines from every part of the world. However, for most people, the hot dog and hamburger duo faithfully represent American cuisine. If we limit ourselves to popular opinion, American cuisine would not have anything particularly original to offer, since the hot dog comes from the German frankfurter and the hamburger, also, comes from Germany.

Three oceans surround this country. There are high mountains, wide rivers and immense expanses of arable land, which provided the necessary resources for the survival of its four founding races. The Amerindians, French, English and Spanish surpassed each other in the art of quickly and simply producing nourishing and flavorful dishes. The diverse peoples who later immigrated to the United States adapted their own recipes to the country's produce and in turn American families quickly adopted their recipes. As a result, the variety in regional American cooking is impressive; the culinary repertoire extends from Louisiana to New Mexico, passing through Chinatown in San Francisco to Little Tokyo in Los Angeles, and from the deserts of Nevada to the dairy lands of New England. As well as recreating a whole range of European and oriental dishes, Americans have created a meal of their own: brunch. A contraction of the words breakfast and lunch, brunch is served at mid-morning. It is a meal where every fantasy is allowed and where everyone can serve himself from among the many dishes arranged on the table.

The dietary habits of Americans have undergone some radical changes during the last few years. After the return to the land movement in the 1970s and the rediscovery of whole grain cereals, America is discovering a leaner cuisine, which focuses more on the nutritional value and presentation of the food than on its quantity. Today, chicken breasts with wild rice, braised celery and lemon sorbet are more popular than the uninspiring casserole recipes featured in the popular magazines and television programs of the last twenty years.

New England Stew
(United States)

Level of Difficulty	
Preparation Time	20 min
Cost per Serving	**$**
Number of Servings	12
Nutritional Value	376 calories 36.1 g protein 7.2 mg iron
Food Exchanges	4 oz meat 2 vegetable exchanges 1/2 bread exchange
Cooking Time	2 h 50 min
Standing Time	None
Power Level	100%, 50%, 70%
Write Your Cooking Time Here ß	

Ingredients
2 kg (4-1/2 lb) corned beef brisket
6 potatoes
2 small rutabagas
6 carrots
1 small cabbage
10 small onions

Method
— Put the beef in a casserole and cover with cold water.
— Cover and cook at 100% for 10 minutes; skim off the fat.
— Set the power level at 50% and continue cooking for 2 hours, or until the meat is tender.
— In the meantime, peel the potatoes and cut them into quarters.
— Peel the rutabagas and cut into cubes.
— Peel and slice the carrots.
— Cut the cabbage into wedges.
— Peel the onions and cut into quarters.
— Add all the vegetables.
— Cover and cook at 100% for 10 minutes; stir.
— Continue cooking at 70% for 20 to 30 minutes, stirring once during the cooking time.
— Strain and serve surrounded by the vegetables.

MICROTIPS

Variations Welcome!

We have just given the typical recipe for New England Stew. However, cooking is a very personal art and all cooks are free to modify recipes as they wish. So, depending on the products available, your supplies or your own preferences, you can easily omit or make substitutions for some of the vegetables. You can use sliced parsnip instead of rutabaga, for example. Different types of onions can add color to your dish. You can make the stew even more attractive by experimenting with the shapes of different vegetables. Use a food processor to cut the carrots into scalloped cubes or rounds. Instead of cutting the onions into quarters slice them or leave them whole.

Any investment you make in the presentation of a dish like this one will pay dividends by making the dish even more appetizing.

Boston Baked Beans (United States)

Level of Difficulty	
Preparation Time	15 min*
Cost per Serving	$
Number of Servings	6
Nutritional Value	392 calories 12.4 g protein 42.8 g carbohydrate
Food Exchanges	3 oz meat 1-1/2 fat exchanges
Cooking Time	3 h
Standing Time	None
Power Level	100%, 50%
Write Your Cooking Time Here	

* Soak the beans in cold water for 12 hours before cooking.

Ingredients
450 g (1 lb) navy beans
50 mL (1/4 cup) molasses
15 mL (1 tablespoon) brown sugar
5 mL (1 teaspoon) dry mustard
5 mL (1 teaspoon) salt
5 mL (1 teaspoon) pepper
1 onion, chopped
115 g (4 oz) salt pork, cubed

Method
— Rinse the beans and put them in a bowl; cover with cold water and leave to soak for 12 hours.
— Cover and cook at 100% for 40 minutes or until boiling.
— Drain the beans and reserve the liquid.
— Put the beans in a casserole and add all the other ingredients; pour in enough of the cooking liquid to cover the mixture.
— Cover and cook at 100% for 20 minutes.
— Stir and continue cooking at 50% for 1-1/2 to 2 hours, stirring several times. Check regularly that the beans are covered with water; if needed add more water.

This traditional recipe is always appreciated. Assemble all the ingredients required before beginning.

Cover the beans with cold water and allow to soak for 12 hours.

Stir after 20 minutes of cooking and continue to cook at 50% for 1-1/2 to 2 hours, stirring several times. Check regularly to make sure that the beans are always covered with liquid; if not, add more water.

97

Quebec: Regional Dishes

Born French, adapting to life in New France, enriched first by Amerindian cuisine and then by the British tradition, Quebec's cuisine has been in constant evolution. Originally heavy and hearty, it has adapted to its people's lifestyle. Urban, sedentary life is less physically demanding than that of the original loggers and settlers and so dietary habits have had to be modified.

Traditionally, Quebec cuisine was rich in fats, meats and sugar. The first Quebeckers were woodsmen who worked long and hard in the cold weather. They drew their energy from bacon, meatball stews, meat pies, pork crackle and headcheese spread on thick slices of homemade bread, often served with baked beans. For a long time their only source of sugar was maple sap (transformed into sugar and syrup by boiling and condensation). Maple sugar was, like corn, the heritage of the Amerindians. Stored in golden brown squares, the stock of maple sugar had to last all year. Maple products were also used to make sugar tarts, eggs cooked in syrup, maple sugar tartlets and maple taffy.

The affection Quebeckers feel for maple products continues to this day. In the springtime many people carry on the tradition of meeting in maple groves to sample the freshest maple syrup, produced right in front of their eyes and spread over crêpes, slices of bread or smoked ham and eggs. And the tradition carries on at home, since visitors to the sugar cabin inevitably bring back several liters of this precious liquid to be enjoyed in the morning with pancakes or used to

Every region of Quebec has its own specialty. Lac–Saint–Jean has its "six pâtés" (the proper name has never been known for sure), an immense pie made with a combination of pork, veal and beef and rabbit, partridge, duck or other game. Preceded by broad bean soup and followed by bread and blueberry pudding, this Sagouine-style meal recalls the meals of the rivermen. The Montérégie area is full of orchards and so it is not surprising to see dishes as roast pork with apples or chicken with cider on the menu. In the Sorel area many restaurants offers *gibelotte,* a sort of bouillabaisse made with local freshwater fish.

Many regions make use of the riches of the sea: Greenland haddock, Arctic char, dory, bass and Matane shrimps. Ouananiche (lake trout) with fennel or cod tongues, for example, are typical recipes from the Lower Saint Lawrence and Gaspé areas that should definitely be sampled.

In the last few years new trends in cooking and agriculture have appeared. Fresh lamb from Quebec has become very popular and quail is becoming much more common as are partridge and pheasant, which some breeders are offering to an ever increasing number of both curious and convinced consummers. Fiddlehead greens, which have only recently been commercially cultivated, and snow crab are also among the new arrivals to the Quebec dinner table.

Seafood Stew (Quebec: Iles de la Madeleine)

Level of Difficulty	🍴🍴
Preparation Time	45 min
Cost per Serving	$ $ $
Number of Servings	8
Nutritional Value	625 calories 38.1 g protein 26.3 g lipids
Food Exchanges	4 oz meat 1/2 vegetable exchange 3 bread exchanges 1-1/2 fat exchanges
Cooking Time	34 min
Standing Time	None
Power Level	70%, 90%, 100%
Write Your Cooking Time Here	

Ingredients
Pastry Crust:
1 L (4 cups) flour
40 mL (8 teaspoons) baking powder
10 mL (2 teaspoons) salt
10 mL (3 teaspoons) dry mustard
15 mL (3 teaspoons) dry parsley
150 mL (2/3 cup) shortening or lard
425 mL (1-3/4 cup) milk

Filling:
500 mL (2 cups) potatoes, diced
250 mL (1 cup) celery, diced
125 mL (1/2 cup) onion, finely chopped
125 mL (1/2 cup) carrots, diced
250 mL (1 cup) water
500 mL (2 cups) scallops
500 mL (2 cups) lobster meat, cut into small pieces
50 mL (1/4 cup) green onions, finely chopped
50 mL (1/4 cup) butter
60 mL (4 tablespoons) cornstarch, dissolved in
375 mL (12.5 oz) can evaporated milk
salt and pepper to taste

Method
— In a bowl, combine the flour, baking powder, salt, dry mustard and parsley.
— Add the shortening or lard and the milk and blend to obtain a smooth dough.
— Roll the dough out to form a rectangle large enough to line the bottom and sides of a 20 cm x 37.5 cm x 7 cm (8 in x 15 in x 3 in) baking dish.
— Cut small fish out of the remaining dough (for garnish).

— Put the dough-lined dish on a raised rack in the oven and cook at 70% for 6 to 7 minutes, giving the dish a half-turn halfway through the cooking time; set the crust aside.
— Put the small fish-shaped pieces of dough onto a plate and place on a raised rack in the oven; cook at 90% for 2 minutes and set aside.
— In a casserole, combine the potatoes, celery, onion, carrots and water; cover and cook at 100% for 4 to 6 minutes, stirring once during the cooking time. Set aside.
— Put the scallops in another dish and cook at 70% for 7 to 9 minutes, stirring twice during the cooking time.
— Add the scallops, lobster, green onions and butter to the vegetables.
— Cover and cook together at 90% for 2 minutes, stirring once during the cooking time.
— Add the cornstarch dissolved in the evaporated milk to the mixture and season.
— Cook at 100% for 7 to 8 minutes, stirring 3 times during the cooking.
— Check the seasoning and adjust if necessary.
— Pour the filling into the crust and garnish with the fish-shaped pastry pieces.

Pigs' Trotters Stew (Quebec)

Level of Difficulty	🍴
Preparation Time	30 min
Cost per Serving	$
Number of Servings	6
Nutritional Value	495 calories 50 g protein 6.9 mg iron
Food Exchanges	5 oz meat 1 bread exchange
Cooking Time	2 h 18 min
Standing Time	None
Power Level	100%, 70%
Write Your Cooking Time Here	

Ingredients
4 to 6 pigs' trotters
1 onion, studded with 4 cloves
1 bay leaf
5 mL (1 teaspoon) pork seasoning
salt and pepper to taste
175 mL (3/4 cup) flour, toasted
250 mL (1 cup) cold water

Meatballs:
675 g (1-1/2 lb) ground pork
1 onion, grated
125 mL (1/2 cup) fresh bread (crusts removed), crumbled
1 egg, beaten
salt and pepper to taste
1 mL (1/4 teaspoon) fine herbs

Method
— Split the rind on the pigs' trotters.
— Put the pigs' trotters in a casserole and cover with hot water.
— Add the onion, bay leaf and the seasonings.
— Cover and cook at 100% for 40 minutes.
— Stir the pigs' trotters.
— Continue cooking at 70% for 40 to 60 minutes, or until the meat comes away easily from the bone.
— Remove the pigs' trotters, bone them and set aside.
— Remove the bay leaf and onion from the cooking liquid.
— Dissolve the toasted flour in the cold water and add, stirring constantly, to the bouillon.
— Cook uncovered at 100% for 15 to 20 minutes, stirring every 5 minutes; set the sauce aside.
— To prepare the meatballs, put the grated onion in a dish and cook, covered, at 100% for 2 to 3 minutes, stirring once during the cooking time.
— Soak the bread in the egg.
— Add the onion and bread to the ground pork; season to taste and add the fine herbs.
— Mix well and shape into meatballs.
— Put the meat from the pigs' trotters and the meatballs into the sauce.
— Cook at 100% for 10 to 15 minutes or until the meatballs are cooked, stirring twice during the cooking time.

Blueberry Pie
(Quebec: Lac-Saint-Jean)

Level of Difficulty	🍴🍴
Preparation Time	30 min
Cost per Serving	$
Number of Servings	8
Nutritional Value	295 calories 46.4 g carbohydrate
Food Exchanges	2 fruit exchanges 2 bread exchanges 1/2 fat exchanges
Cooking Time	14 min
Standing Time	None
Power Level	70%, 90%, 100%
Write Your Cooking Time Here	

MICROTIPS

Choosing Blueberries

Cultivated blueberries are larger and sweeter than wild blueberries, but the wild variety are better for pies. Whether buying or picking, choose plump fruit, of equal size, with their leaves removed.

Ingredients
500 mL (2 cups) blueberries
2 single pie crusts
pinch cinnamon
pinch sugar
250 mL (1 cup) sugar
15 mL (1 tablespoon) flour
15 mL (1 tablespoon) cornstarch

Method
— Line a pie plate with one of the crusts.
— Pierce the bottom with a fork in several places.
— Put the pie plate on a raised rack in the oven and cook at 70% for 4 to 6 minutes, giving the dish a half-turn halfway through the cooking time.
— Let cool.
— Cut the other crust into strips and arrange them in a crisscross pattern on a sheet of waxed papper.
— Sprinkle the strips with the sugar and cinnamon.
— Put the sheet of waxed paper on a raised rack in the oven and cook the strips of dough at 90% for 2 minutes.
— Let cool.
— Gently combine the blueberries, sugar, flour and cornstarch.
— Cook at 100% for 4 to 6 minutes, stirring carefully twice during the cooking time.
— Pour the mixture into the pie crust.
— Arrange the strips of cooked dough over the pie.

Across the World

This overview of international cuisine is just a glimpse of the thousand and one culinary possibilities to be explored across many centuries and continents. We are aware that we have just touched on, for example, the richness and complexity of the many countries of the Far East. Although oriental cuisine is the subject of an entire volume in the *Microwave Magic* series, to supplement our coverage in this, international, volume we should like to say a few more words about the cuisine of two oriental countries whose culinary culture is particularly important: Vietnam and Japan.

Vietnamese Cuisine

Delicacy. This is the main characteristic of the culture, cuisine and people of this country, a neighbor of China, a coastal country surrounded by two seas rich in products as exotic as they are varied and nourishing. Vietnamese cuisine is not simply a variation on Chinese cooking; sweet smelling, suave and subtle, it plays on aromas and flavors with consummate art.

Whether for the Tet Festival (the Vietnamese New Year) or simply for a family supper, the Vietnamese meal usually begins with a soup, either corn or asparagus, or a simple bouillon enhanced with a few slices of a colorful vegetable. In Vietnam, an especially light soup will often replace the beverage during the meal. The only drink suggested is sake (rice wine) since any other wine would mask the flavor and subtle combination of Vietnamese foods.

The fertile rice paddies which line the interminable shores of the Mekong, the great southern river of this long and narrow country, provide the rice that is the basis of the Vietnamese diet. There are many different types of rice in Vietnam and a multitude of simple dishes and varied recipes derived from it. Cooking rice is an art and a science that the Vietnamese have refined over centuries.

Some foods are always a part of the daily diet—rice cakes (thin, round sheets made with dried rice flour) compete with thin, transparent noodles prepared with soya flour. *Nuoc-mam* sauce, made from a brine prepared with small saltwater fish and salt, is to Vietnamese cooking what soy sauce is to Chinese cooking. As well as this national condiment, a whole range of spice are used, ginger probably being the most common, cinnamon, both in powder and sticks, and lemon balm, used to flavor beef and chicken dishes, following close behind. In fact, Vietnamese sauces, such as *nuoc-mam,* are used as we in the West use salt and pepper—they are always on the table.

Vietnamese cuisine makes use of all of nature's bounty to perfume its dishes. The flavor of a soup is enhanced by a few dried lilies, also called "golden needles." In other dishes, lotus grains are used as seasoning or water chestnuts and bamboo shoots may be added to bolster a simple recipe. Basic foods, such as eggs and mushrooms, are often prepared together and garnished with coconut and bamboo shoots. Chicken, peanuts, cinnamon pâté, tofu (a vegetable cheese made with fermented soy milk) and more complex foods, such as simmered pork hock with lemon balm or duck with cane sugar, are some examples of the many ingredients used in this cuisine.

The choice of desserts, from coconut cream to flambéed bananas and cake cooked in banana leaves, confirms the Vietnamese ability to combine everyday necessities with the poetry of a superb country. The names of many dishes, such as Chicken with Jade Rice Hidden in the Mountain and Trembling Beef are proof of this fact.

Japanese Cuisine
The inhabitants of Japan, the country of the rising sun, have long demonstrated their refinement and their aesthetic sense. The virtues of their cuisine cannot be doubted: distinguished, flavorful, healthy, nutritious and colorful, they combine culinary good sense with good looks. Why is Japanese cooking so healthy? First of all, because it contains very little fat and cholesterol since its main sources of protein are fish, shellfish and soy derivatives such as tofu rather than meat. Another important aspect of Japanese cuisine is in the freshness of vegetables, which include Chinese cabbage, eggplant, shallots, chives, bamboo shoots, mushrooms, lotus roots, spinach, carrots and snow peas. These vegetables are used abundantly and, along with a small amount of fish or meat, will feed a large number of people at a relatively low cost. Vegetables are also rich in fiber, vitamins and minerals, which are essential to a healthy diet. Finally, Japanese cooking methods traditionally require very little fat and . . . very little time.

Many Japanese dishes, such as sashimi (thinly sliced raw fish), require little or no cooking. The natural flavors and odors of these foods are thus intact, as are their colors and textures. Japanese cooking is mainly known for its large international successes such as tempura and sukiyaki. But a more in-depth exploration of this cuisine has resulted in an appreciation of sushi, made with flavored rice shaped into small cakes and topped or wrapped with such garnishes as pieces of raw fish, eggs or vegetables.

Japanese meals generally start with soup. The best-known soups are undoubtedly the clear bouillons garnished with a beautiful pink shrimp or a few vegetables, such as carrots, white radishes or lightly cooked okra. Soy sauce, or tamari, the origin of which goes back 2500 years, is a well-known condiment. It is a central element of Japanese seasoning and a true national symbol. Another national symbol is the traditional Japanese beverage; sake, a rice wine consumed warm or cold, depending on the food with which it is served. If not sake, a glass of hot green tea will complete a Japanese meal beautifully.

The Gourmet Globe Trotter's Glossary

Cassata: An Italian ice cream with candied fruit made in a rectangular mold.

Chutney: A sweet and sour condiment made with fruits and vegetables cooked in a sugared vinegar.

Curry: An Indian seasoning, usually composed of chili, turmeric, cumin, coriander and other spices. This term also designates a dish prepared with this seasoning.

Imperial roll: A Chinese recipe for a filling wrapped in flaky pastry, also called a spring roll because it is often served at festivals to mark the beginning of spring.

Lichee: A Chinese fruit the size of a prune, covered with a rough pink or red skin.

Marzipan: A decorative sweet made with crushed almonds, sugar and egg whites, with added coloring and often shaped to resemble fruits and vegetables. Used extensively in Germany.

Merguez: A sausage, fried or grilled, made with beef and lamb and seasoned with red pepper, which gives it its characteristic color.

Moussaka: A popular dish in Turkey and Greece, made with sliced eggplant arranged in layers alternately with ground lamb and covered with a tomato sauce.

Norwegian omelette: A dessert made with ice cream arranged on an angel food cake base, covered with meringue and heated in the oven before being flambéed.

Ouzo: A colorless Greek liqueur flavored with the essence of anise.

Conversion Chart

**Conversion Chart for the
Main Measures Used in
Cooking**

Volume
1 teaspoon............ 5 mL
1 tablespoon........ 15 mL

1 quart (4 cups)....... 1 litre
1 pint (2 cups)....... 500 mL
1/2 cup............ 125 mL
1/4 cup............ 50 mL

Weight
2.2 lb......... 1 kg (1000 g)
1.1 lb............... 500 g
0.5 lb............... 225 g
0.25 lb.............. 115 g

1 oz................. 30 g

**Metric Equivalents
for Cooking
Temperatures**

49°C............... 120°F
54°C............... 130°F
60°C............... 140°F
66°C............... 150°F
71°C............... 160°F
77°C............... 170°F
82°C............... 180°F
93°C............... 200°F
107°C.............. 225°F

120°C............... 250°F
135°C............... 275°F
150°C............... 300°F
160°C............... 325°F
180°C............... 350°F
190°C............... 375°F
200°C............... 400°F
220°C............... 425°F
230°C............... 450°F

Readers will note that, in the recipes, we give 250 mL as the equivalent for 1 cup and 450 g as the equivalent for 1 lb and that fractions of these measurements are even less mathematically accurate. The reason for this is that mathematically accurate conversions are just not practical in cooking. Your kitchen scales are simply not accurate enough to weigh 454 g—the true equivalent of 1 lb—and it would be a waste of time to try. The conversions given in this series, therefore, necessarily represent approximate equivalents, but they will still give excellent results in the kitchen. No problems should be encountered if you adhere to either metric or imperial measurements throughout a recipe.

Index

MICROTIPS